FOR THE **LOVE** OF
Real Estate
TALES FROM THE TRENCHES

SHARON MASON

in·fluence
PARTNERS IN PUBLISHING

Published by Sharon Mason Media
in partnership with Influence Publishing Inc., March 2022
ISBN: 978-1-7776091-0-8

Editing: Lee Robinson
Book and Cover Design: Tara Eymundson
Cover Photo: David Naman Photography

Dedication

After much consideration, I decided to dedicate this book
to my father, the late Lorrace Eric Kirk, aka "Lorrie."
He led the way as the first entrepreneur in the Kirk family
and was a big inspiration into who I am today as a real
estate agent and as a person of integrity and ethics.

FOR THE LOVE OF THE AUTHOR

Testimonials

"Finally! A book that takes you through the real estate industry and shows you the true ups and downs. This book is the real deal! It not only takes you through the industry but also guides you through everyday life lessons. It is an honour to know and learn from Sharon herself. As the owner and founder of BEA Real Estate Assistant Course, I will definitely make this a must read with my students."

Bernadette Singh
Entrepreneur
Owner and Founder of Bringing Education Alive

"In *For the Love of Real Estate—Tales from the Trenches*, Sharon shares her journey of travelling the winding and sometimes bumpy road of life as a realtor and draws us all in through her entertaining stories and lessons, causing many a chuckle as the pages turn. Through her book, Sharon selflessly gives away her heart for all that wish to receive it. I have had the greatest blessing and privilege to know Sharon for the past fifteen years and to experience her heart—which is full of love, resilience, grace, entrepreneurship, generosity, adventure, humour and passion! What a gift she has to offer!

"As I read through the pages, I gleaned so many golden nuggets of truth, insight, encouragement and wisdom—and I'm not even a realtor! This is Sharon at her vintage best and is a book I will gratefully share with my colleagues, friends and anyone considering the worthy and high calling of a realtor."

Yvonne Hogenes
Owner of Malary's Fashion Network
Recipient of both the Surrey Board of Trade Business Person of the Year Award and the Woman Entrepreneur Award

"This is a must-read. With heartfelt stories, Sharon shares the ins and outs of being passionate about what it takes to be successful in real estate and maintain integrity and heart. At the forefront of every teaching is Sharon's heart and care for the people who work with her. People may look at the title and think it is only for budding real estate agents but that is only part of it. Entrepreneurs who read the jewels in this book will learn principles about what is important in building a successful business. It's not about the sale; it's about making connections with people and building strong relationships first, and the money will follow. Well done, Sharon!"

Cyndy Greeno
Master Career and Life Coach
Mentor of the Year, as recognized by the Career Development Association of British Columbia

"This book is so engaging that when I came to the last chapter, I wished there were more chapters! It ended before I was ready to have it end!"

Anna Garnett
Head of Business Development
Canadian Tenant Inspection Services

"The incredible stories that are woven throughout this book teach wisdom and life lessons of value to anyone—realtor or not. In a refreshing style, the author shares her candid discoveries of personal growth through honesty, humility, love and laughter. I could feel her natural light shine through these pages just the same way she lights up a room. If you want to learn from one of the best in the business, jump on for a fascinating ride and a good read."

Cindi Knight
Elite award-winning realtor over three decades
Century 21 All Star Realty, Edmonton, Alberta

"Sharon Mason has been an inspiration to us in real estate since we first met her in the mid–80s. She is taking a continuous pulse of the market daily, and she shares her informed analysis with colleagues and clients alike. Reading this book will give you a sense of how to be a successful realtor and will share some life lessons with you as well. Sharon is a strong believer in mentorship, and she is as willing to learn as she is to teach. If you are looking at a future as a realtor or are looking for a realtor to represent you, this is a must-read."

Jim Garnett
Founder and President
Canadian Tenant Inspection Services

"Are you saving for your first home? Selling your home? Downsizing? Maybe you love the idea of being a realtor? Thinking of a career change? STOP! Before you make any one of these life-changing decisions—READ THIS BOOK! Sharon Mason has written the one must-read book for anyone buying, selling or making a career choice. Everyone needs to read her life lessons and become an assured buyer or seller. Sit with Sharon at your own kitchen table and learn from her forty years of award-willing experience as an outstanding, integrous and successful realtor. Written as a delightful conversation, Sharon will educate you and make sure the biggest financial decisions of your life go well!"

Mary Pichette
Mother, business owner over thirty-five years, award-winning leader in the non-profit sector, former Criminology professor, trainer, speaker and contributing author of No. 1 bestselling book on Amazon, Women of Worth—Power, Passion and Purpose

Testimonials

"While my mom was writing this book (during a recent pandemic lockdown) in a mere six week, I said to her, 'I think you are writing the book for me, Mummy!' I was, at that time, studying to get my real estate licence. I now realize that this book is for EVERYONE. Whether you are interested in real estate or not, this book will entertain you and while you're laughing, teach you about relationships, about leading with love and about BEING in the world."

Justine Priestley
Author's daughter and a new realtor (2021)

"Over the years, Sharon has helped me to sell and buy a total of eight times. As a person who has had no experience with business matters, I have always told Sharon how grateful I am to have an agent who takes the time and has the words to make it all clear to me."

Vera Harrison

"As we all know, selling or buying a home can be a very stressful, but Sharon made this time much less stressful for us, especially the sale of our home during the covid pandemic. Sharon is very professional, positive, friendly and patient. We could not have asked for a better realtor. One of the most revealing aspects of dealing with Sharon was the time she openly suggested that we keep our home and rent it out instead of selling it! I replied that she would then lose a sale. Her answer was that it was more important for us to explore all of our viable options. I cannot thank you enough, Sharon, for everything you have done for us. You are the absolute best!"

Clive and Tracey M.

"We have bought or sold properties with Sharon four times now. We kept coming back to her for her in-depth industry knowledge, extensive experience and professionalism. We also appreciate her attentiveness and patience in walking us through the nitty-gritty of the whole buying and selling process and in addressing questions or concerns we had. We felt confident with her abilities and greatly enjoyed working with her for her warmth, sincerity and good humour. She made the whole process smoother and less intimidating. We highly recommend her to anyone."

Louis and Michelle

"Sharon and Al Mason are most knowledgeable and highly professional. We met them at an open house they were hosting. Within a few minutes of general enquires, we got this amazing feeling that they truly understood our needs, our budget and our desires. We were excited to be working with them as soon as they accepted us as their clients. Upon every house viewing, Sharon made a list of pros and cons, which made it extremely easy for us to decide if we wanted to proceed to the next step. Our dream home that we own today was made possible due to Sharon's experience and realtor friendships she has built over the years. Our seller's realtor was eager to work with Sharon, in spite of dealing with multiple offers. Sharon's skillful negotiations resulted in us getting this wonderful home which has fulfilled our desires and much more. We purchased, moved in and settled down in our home during the pandemic, all possible through Sharon and Al's expert guidance and assurance that everything would be well in the end."

Anu S.

"When it came time to downsize, there was no question who our realtor would be. Sharon had helped us purchase our home in 1984! It was a difficult time of life, but Sharon stood by us as she always does, caring most about the clients and the experience they are having. With her, it's never just about the sale—far from it! In fact, Sharon's integrity, commitment and caring attitude make her a great asset to her profession. Sharon, I would not be where I am today without having you beside me every step of the way."

Lorraine J.

"The whole experience with Sharon just naturally flowed. Her positive attitude, sunny personality and knowledge of the real estate market gave us a great deal of confidence. She kept on top of the prices in the market and readily made adjustments as prices were rising instead of pricing to flip. From our first meeting, Sharon guided us through the whole process, was very detailed in explaining each step of the way and promptly answered any questions that came up. She really works with the owners and goes beyond her call of duty. She sets the bar high to get the house prepared for showing, and in our case, she was most helpful in providing some props for a media room that was empty. It was a great collaboration and experience from start to finish. A standout quality we noticed was she was very good in closing our sale, following through with inspection and communicating to realtors and their clients. Sharon builds great relationships and works from the heart, which is why she is so successful and trustworthy! We would definitely recommend her to our family and friends."

Gerry and Tracy D.

"We met Sharon Mason by chance. We were looking for an agent to sell our house, and our mortgage rep at the bank recommended her. Once we met Sharon and Al—her chauffeur, sidekick and life partner—we were hooked. Sharon is truly devoted to getting her clients a sale they are happy with. Her caring, professional attitude makes you feel like you asked your best friend to sell your house. I would not hesitate for a moment to recommend Sharon to any of my family or friends. Sharon will do whatever is necessary to get the sale done, all the while keeping the best interests of her clients first and foremost. If you want your house sold and want it done in a timely, professional manner, ask Sharon to list it."

Steve and Robbie S.

Testimonials

"Sharon was referred to us by a neighbour when other agents had not been able to get an offer on our condo. We had made an offer subject to the sale of it, and the townhouse we wanted to buy was necessary to our plan of having George's elderly mother come live with us. Sharon explained to us the importance of correct pricing, how that and only that would generate showings and interest. The market was slow, and we had been for sale for months. On her advice, we priced it $5,000 below the other condos in our building, and there were a lot of them. We got an offer in three weeks, but it was far below what we needed to buy the townhouse. Sharon went to bat for us, and she and the agent handling the townhouse project were able to convince the developer to take less for the townhouse. We agreed that he would install less deluxe appliances in return. We needed to get our mother living with us as soon as possible, and we were all moved in within forty-five days. We never dreamed that having the right agent could make such a difference. Thank you, Sharon. We had almost given up."

George and Jean McKenzie

"Sharon is a charming, wise and graceful woman, while at the same time very tenacious. As her book explores all the trials and tribulations through her career, it also showcases the many relationships nurtured by her that continue on today. I loved reading every page of this book and highly recommend it not only to realtors new to the business but also to any seasoned realtor or anyone interested in a good read and some laughs. I respect Sharon very much and love being part of her team. I am so proud to call Sharon not only a mentor but also my friend."

Joanne M.

Owner of Ocean Breeze Staging Consulting

"Over the years, it has been my pleasure, and financially my good fortune, to have had Sharon Mason as my realtor. I have purchased two homes and sold one with Sharon as my guide. When it comes to real estate and the ever-changing markets and trends, I believe nothing beats years of solid experience in the business, and Sharon has this in spades! She is both honest and straightforward in her approach. Sharon is a real family person who values integrity and respect. Yet at the same time she is able to be a strong negotiator too. Buying and selling a house can be a stressful and, at times, a very emotional journey, and this is where Sharon lends not only her years of business acumen but also her truly intuitive sense of compassion, humor and understanding. She has great communication skills and is able to use these skills in negotiations to get the very best offer for her clients. It gives me great pleasure to recommend Sharon Mason as a realtor you can not only trust to get the job done, but also a realtor that you will enjoy working with—a genuine caring person who really does have your best interests at heart."

Barbara O.

Contents

Acknowledgements

Becoming a published author is quite an experience—a daunting task on many levels. It involves going public and "putting it on the line," so to speak. I found that it took a lot of "getting ready," and the getting ready was 100% me discussing it with myself inside my own head.

One big conclusion I came to is that I am standing on a lot of people's shoulders. No one "gets there" on their own. "There" can mean many things depending on one's individual journey. For me, my ancestors were part of pioneering this country, and each generation provided a better life and more education for the next one. They came from France, England, Scotland, Ireland and America. My paternal great grandmother, Nancy Bellerose Killips, was Metis and my maternal grandmother, Juanita Gillette Townsend, was American. The blend of cultures and communities has made us all the stronger. So, in memory of all of you who went before, I acknowledge my ancestral family and my recent and immediate family for the generational legacy that brought me to this sacred place where the legacy lives on.

Other "shoulders" I want to acknowledge and give all due respect and gratitude to are all my teachers and mentors, with special recognition to the late Dr. Gordon R. Stacey, a brilliant counsellor, a man of faith, a life coach and a dear friend, who founded the well-known and respected Union Gospel Mission in Vancouver. Thank you for always believing in me and supporting me to be courageous in embracing and sharing my talents and gifts.

In my real estate life, I can only attempt to include everyone who has contributed to me and, therefore, to this book. The amazing company known as Realty World played a huge part in my success and growth both in business and as a human being. Thank you to Cora

Toth, the late Harold Waddell and the excellent staff. Your corporate culture was a treasure.

Thanks to Chris O'Toole, the owner of the Realty World franchise where I came of age and rose to the top. You taught me to swim with the sharks and not get eaten. Your focus on personal growth, correct thinking and achievement in life created a winning team that brought much glory and satisfaction to your organization. A big thank you to Gord Pipkey, who was our manager and resident mortgage broker back in the day. You helped me enormously and in so many ways. Thanks for the recognition and kindness we all came to appreciate from you. Then there's my dear friend, Tim Timmath, a real estate rock star and a perfect example of dedicated leadership. You were a great manager and friend, always leading with humility and patience. You made me believe! May you enjoy your much deserved retirement. You will be missed.

Then there's the Bock family! The late Barry Bock, also a shining star as a realtor, our company owner, a superb manager and dear friend: I miss him every day. To Barry's wife, Jane, and daughter, Rachel, who recently took ownership of our HomeLife franchise: Thanks for carrying on a fine legacy of integrity and continuing excellence in creating a fine working environment. In fact, we are a "business family" in so many ways.

I also want to take a moment to acknowledge some of the thought leaders who have influenced me through their books, CDs and motivational presentations. I recommend that anyone interested in a better business and personal life tune in to the works of Jim Rohn and Steven Covey, both of whom changed my life. Floyd Wickman saved me with his training and taught me how to "do my magic." I cannot forget "the classics" by Dr. Norman Vincent Peale, Dale Carnegie, Earl Nightingale, Napoleon Hill, Jack Canfield and Zig Ziglar, to name a few.

Then there's my publisher, Julie Ann Salisbury, founder and pres-

Acknowledgements

ident of Influence Publishing, and editor, Lee Robinson. Thanks for putting up with my technological and digital fumbles and for your endless patience while I pulled all the bits and pieces together that are so important in supporting the book itself. I had so much to learn (and still do) and am eternally grateful for your wisdom and generosity.

Special recognition to Adrienne Kakoullis, president of Rise PR, for her amazing contribution to getting the word out about the book and the story behind it. Words are not adequate to express my appreciation and gratitude.

Thanks very much to all my friends and colleagues who read enough of my manuscript to write an endorsement: Jim and Anna Garnett, Yvonne Hogenes, Cindy Greeno, Joanne MacKay, Cindi Knight, Bernadette Singh, Mary Pichette and my daughter, Justine. To my dear clients who have written dozens of testimonials for me: I had to choose a few for the book, and it wasn't easy. I appreciate you all for your ongoing support.

David Naman, photographer "par excellence," you honour me by agreeing to photograph me for the cover. I never dreamed of having an international award-winning photographer take my photo! Star power for sure. Many thanks also to Yvonne Hogenes, multiple award winner for business, entrepreneurship and philanthropy and owner of Malary's Fashion Network. Another honour for me was to have you help me with wardrobe. What can you say about a lady like Jacqueline Jongkind, makeup artiste par excellence! Thank you for helping so beautifully with my face! I am blessed to have such friends, and you know I am always here for you!

Then there's my family. First and foremost is my husband, Al Mason. You are my rock and biggest supporter in so many ways. Al and my beloved daughter, Justine Priestley, have read every word as it came off the printer and have made great suggestions and given me the courage to find what I hope is my "voice" and to keep going forward. You always make me feel like I have something worth saying and worth offering to the world. Now for my son, Jason Priestley: I can never thank you enough for your insightful foreword and the perspective that you share in it. I acknowledge you for your wisdom and broad vision regarding our collective journey as a family. I am so proud of you and your sister. You are both outstanding people, and I am grateful to be sharing this life with you.

Lastly, I want to thank the many friends, family, colleagues and clients who have kept asking the question, "Sharon, when are you going to write your book?" Some might call it nagging... I call it support! I hope you enjoy it. I am standing on your shoulders too!

In gratitude and service,

Sharon Mason

Foreword

When my mother asked me to write a foreword for her book, I was honored. Of course I was honored, as any son would be, to have the opportunity to write some kind words about the fine work of literature his mother had painstakingly written and was now publishing for the world to enjoy.

My mom told me she had written a book about real estate, her experiences in that profession and important lessons for the potential realtor reader. The book that follows is, in fact, something much more personal.

Yes, *For the Love of Real Estate* is about real estate, about buying and selling real estate, but it is also an autobiography and a self-help book of sorts. For my mother, selling real estate is more than just the transaction of selling or buying a home; she believes that real estate is about personal relationships and cultivating those relationships for a long time. And in order to have long-term relationships, you need to be a certain type of person, and a certain type of friend.

My mother began her real estate career in the early '80s. I was just a teenager back then, but I understood the big chance she was taking. She was changing her career, as a middle-aged woman, with no safety net. Being a realtor is a high-risk, high-reward proposition, and it takes a certain kind of person to take on that kind of profession.

And, as you will see in *For the Love of Real Estate*, she, of course, understood the risks she was taking, and felt every bit of pressure that went along with those risks. She acted with great forethought, understanding the ramifications but knowing what she had to do, what she knew in her heart was best for her and her children. She was courageous and she was bold. These were difficult times for our family. But my mother was a warrior; she was the glue that held us all together. My mother did not crumble under the pressure. In fact, she thrived under it and, following in her father's footsteps, went on to have an incredibly successful real estate career.

I watched my mother ascend to the top ranks of the real estate industry through her hard work, grit and determination. And what has kept her there are her qualities that make any business person successful: knowledge, accuracy, honesty, initiative, consistency, dependability and energy. My mother has always acted with purpose and conviction. She is willful, and she is strong. She is also caring and compassionate.

I am very proud of what my mother has accomplished not only in business but also in life, and now with *For the Love of Real Estate*. As she is approaching the start of her ninth decade on this planet, she shows no signs of slowing down. She has built an incredibly happy and full life for herself and her loving husband and continues to inspire members of our family to enter the real estate industry along with her.

I hope *For the Love of Real Estate* inspires you as well.

Jason Priestley
International Award-Winning Actor, Director and Producer

Sharon and her son Jason Priestly at his fiftieth birthday party in Los Angeles.
The theme of the event was "movies of the 1930s and 1940s" (hence the wardrobe).

Introduction

What do we know for sure? I mean *really* for sure!

For myself, I've had a lot of opinions that have proven not to be for sure, but there is one thing I do know: Nothing is ever what it appears to be from the outside looking in. This statement would most certainly include the real estate industry. This book takes you, dear reader, into that world, into my real estate world including the stories, the experiences, the lessons and the reality of what goes on inside this complex and fascinating profession. Whether you are a realtor, a wannabe realtor or a member of society, this book is written for you.

My main desire is to reveal the journey and experiences, issues and complexities, and that no two transactions, sales or purchases are ever the same and are, in fact, unique to the individuals involved. More moving parts than you can imagine! And always a learning curve.

I also desire to humanize our role as realtors—the career realtors who represent the professionalism and leadership provided by the vast majority of my colleagues and myself. The real estate profession is one that quite often gets unjustly vilified by the media and by those members of the public who follow negativity and gossip as if it were real news. The unfortunate and inaccurate way that television and film regularly portray realtors as pushy, insensitive and manipulative provides fodder for the ongoing misinformation the public is fed. This issue applies to many other worthy professions as well. It is my wish and hope that this book will inject balance and a dose of reality into that area of mistaken beliefs. Yes, there are the inevitable bad apples in every barrel, but only a few.

After much prodding from family, friends and clients, I finally decided to overcome the many fears and doubts and to take the plunge and write this book.

I plunged. Obviously!

My wonderful publisher said something the first time we met which became the tipping point in my decision.

She said, "Sharon, it's your legacy."

That brief statement filled in a blank for me. She told me I simply must leave behind the lessons and wisdom I had gained over the decades. Perhaps it was even a sacred duty.

With that lofty notion afloat, all I can do is pledge my best.

So here we go...

1

So Ya Wannabe a Realtor?

"A journey of a thousand miles begins with a single step."
Lao Tzu

"I've always thought about being a realtor! I just love looking at houses!"

I've heard this statement so many times over the years, said by folks who obviously have never seen some of the houses I've marketed and sold!

The houses we "love to look at"? New homes, show homes, street of dreams, properties staged and ready for market under the supervision of a realtor who knows how to quarterback the situation! Yes, they are gorgeous and inspiring, but that's not the whole story.

I blessedly have my expert home stager standing by to give her wise advice and counsel. This amazing lady, Joanne MacKay, always makes my job easier. I provide a complimentary staging consultation which never fails to attract more buyers and a higher sale price. Her company is Ocean Breeze Staging and Colour Consultation. I appreciate her immensely as part of my team.

Some of the properties we realtors see remind me of that classic line "What a dump!" delivered by Bette Davis in the classic film *Beyond the Forest*. That broad could really deliver a line! And that particular line has haunted me more than once in my career—black mould, leaking roofs, peeling paint, dirt and grime, clutter beyond imagination, too much or too little furniture, too stinky, rebellious tenants…I could go on.

Fortunately, most of the time it's not so extreme, just normal well-lived-in properties.

Looking at houses is important but definitely not where the major work lies. Being a realtor includes many moving parts and aspects that are little known to those not involved. It utilizes a complex set of skills and knowledge covering a vast amount of material, including people and communication skills, intuition, dimensions of character, and the ability to handle adversity and manage emotions—not only on a personal level but those of our clients. It also takes intellect, study habits, attention to detail and, last but not least, an entrepreneurial spirit. And that's just for starters. I know it sounds like a lot, but if it's meant for you, it's worth climbing that mountain!

In other words, loving to look at houses isn't enough, but it could be the start of something big.

"Realtors have it easy."

Now there's a notion that's worth unpacking.

It can look like all we do is dress well (except for those who don't!), drive a nice car, put up a 'For Sale' sign, hold an open house (maybe) and take lots of money to the bank. Nothing could be further from the truth.

The first project is deciding to get your real estate licence. Should you or shouldn't you? There are a lot of questions you ought to ask. Take an aptitude test, listen to your intuition and, above all, read this book!

If you're already a realtor and want to survive and thrive…read this book!

The mere act of getting a real estate licence can be a daunting task for many folks. In my jurisdiction, it involves a business school course at the University of British Columbia (which can take several months) followed by a three-hour exam. We are told that roughly 30% of the students pass on their first try. That looks like a 70% failure rate! Not for the faint of heart nor the lazy, that's for sure. And for those who fail, there is then a waiting period before you spend more money to take the exam for a second time.

In BC it costs about $5,000 to take the course, pass the exam and take the required training classes so that you can become licensed for the first two years of your career. Next comes more courses and studies—mandatory courses like Legal Update, Understanding Agency, Ethics, Money Laundering and more. And that's just for starters. It never ends if you want to keep your licence.

Like I said, if this is for you, it's all worth it, and you will be a better person for it.

The hard part is the personal growth. In fact, at times your career will seem like a personal growth program which may or may not have a paycheque attached to it. You will discover amazing things about yourself and others, and you will be challenged indeed. But remember, if this is for you, it's all worth it!

I personally see the role of a dedicated realtor as a "calling." You are in service to your clients. As it is for a doctor, the first rule is "Do no harm." Our job is to educate, advise and protect the public. There will always be those who don't abide by that Golden Rule, but the road to real success lies in dedication and integrity—being the very best you.

Next is making sure you can survive financially while you get established.

"Realtors make tons of money."

Here is another myth worth busting!

Yes we can earn significant amounts of cash, but unfortunately we don't get to keep it all. We earn it, and then it gets distributed to create income for the many:

a. Sharing with the other realtor: In most cases there are two realtors involved—one representing the seller and the other representing the buyer. The split is almost fifty-fifty. Then each realtor must share with his broker in a variety of possible ways.

b. Sharing with your broker: All realtors in every jurisdiction I am aware of must be licensed under the umbrella of a real estate broker. The broker must be licensed and fully accredited to provide certain services (including supervision and oversight) to realtors who sign a contract with their brokerage, and the broker will share in the earnings of the realtors. So, every time I help my clients buy or sell a property, my broker makes money. (Fair enough. My brokers give me tremendous service and value, and I am pleased to assist them to stay in business. Thank you, Jane and Rachel Bock!) There are percentages that go to the owner of any brokerage as "splits" and/or "desk fees." Brokerages can vary greatly in what they offer and the financial arrangements available to realtors.

c. Then there are real estate board fees, association fees like Canadian Real Estate Association, franchise fees, technology fees, charitable donations, social fund, multiple listing service (MLS) fees, advertising, and websites. Lots of deductions.

d. Then come other items such as marketing, entertainment,

an annual client party, your computer and smart phone, technology apps, automobile, business cards, signage, maintaining one's image and so on.

e. Taxes: At least we have lots of tax write-offs! See a–d above.

It's expensive to be a realtor. Back in my heyday, prior to everything being online, it could be even more expensive. We had to do newspaper and magazine advertising. I was paying around $40,000 per year to the Real Estate Weekly and more to other publications. Mind you, I always had a lot of listings to advertise. It got the phone to ring. Nowadays folks find us online, and we are paying for all those services. Times have changed with the digital world, but all fees go nowhere but up, and it's no different for other entrepreneurs and self-employed people like us.

Personally, these days I hope to hang onto forty cents on the dollar which needs to provide for our retirement, living expenses, educating the kids…the usual. The thing with real estate is that I determine how much I earn. Not a boss, not a union…me. Now that's pretty exciting!

So, let's talk about how much realtors really earn. You first need to imagine that it takes various amounts of time to satisfy the needs of a client, including how long it takes to follow up before a client chooses a realtor.

The longest I have ever kept in touch with a client before they asked me to help them sell? Twelve years.

The shortest time I have ever helped someone buy a home? Four days. It was a family referred to me by their realtor in another city. They had sold their home, and the husband was transferred to start a new job in my city, all in two weeks.

One long-time client, a dear lady, loves to tease me, "Wow you realtors make so much money! You must be making fifty cents an hour on me." Needless to say, selling her lovely home took many steps over a period of two and a half years. Maybe it was less than fifty cents an hour, now that I think of it.

LIFE LESSON: Behind every stereotype, generalization or myth, there is a story that will very likely dispel that belief, opinion or attitude.

The following is one of those stories. Let's go back in time to when I was a wannabe realtor…

In 1983 I was thirty-nine years old and about to turn forty. In those days, people always said that "life begins at forty." Hmmm…I guessed I had better get on with it. Now don't get me wrong, I had lived a big life, but one thing was missing—getting paid what I was worth! You know that joke where one guy asks another guy, "What lifestyle would you like to be able to afford?" And he answers, "The one I'm living!"

I had dreams of travel and other luxuries that were not in my financial reach, and I thought of what a difference an extra $20,000 a year would make to my family. After some consideration, I decided on real estate, which was not an idea that came completely out of the blue. My dad was a realtor. In fact, he was an amazing realtor. I observed my family go from rags to riches. I took it for granted at the time, as kids and inexperienced young adults can, but obviously my subconscious mind was recording and absorbing a lot of information. "Kids learn what they observe," as they say, and I was observing and recording and figuring out a lot of stuff without knowing it. Dad would teach me things and tell me stories, and at the end of the day it must have taken root and germinated in there, ultimately in my soul, and when the time came—bingo!—I made a choice that turned out to be so very right.

Now I say, "I'm in real estate, and real estate is in me." And I mean it.

So, $20,000 a year…that was a lot of moolah back in the '80s and '90s! Little did I know that more than $20,000 *a month* was in my future, but there was a road I would have to first travel, an unknown road with potholes, narrow shoulders, deep ditches and sometimes no line down the centre.

I talked to some real estate brokers and managers and got all sorts of info and responses. I was looking for something to resonate with, and I was not finding it. Then someone told me about a company called Realty World and a wonderful lady named Cora Toth who was teaching the UBC real estate course. I needed to be sponsored by a real estate brokerage, and something just felt and sounded right when I looked into the company and spoke to someone at head office. I found the nearest Realty World office and got sponsored. It would turn out to be one of the best decisions I ever made. Then I started the real estate course.

It was a long drive one night per week for six months to a four-hour class. Weekly assignments had to be delivered to UBC—a long drive or a large courier bill. (No email yet.) It also meant having a meaningful relationship with a financial calculator and stressing about passing the exam, which was reportedly gruelling and quite intimidating with a high failure rate. (In fact, I confided in very few friends about my real estate studies in case I failed the exam.)

I was stepping into a huge unknown area, and it felt like jumping off a cliff. It just felt risky and why shouldn't it? I got a study partner and got on with it. And I passed the exam! Whew!

LIFE LESSON: Believe in yourself and hold the vision. You never know what you may achieve or learn.

Soon I found myself in an environment I had never been in before. In my office, I met realtors who were earning six figures. I had never dreamed of anything like that. I quickly realized that the difference between me and them was that they knew stuff I hadn't learned…yet. The operative word being YET. So I set about learning. One thing about me? I am coachable! I encourage you to pursue this characteristic no matter what you're doing: be coachable. Be a sponge, learn stuff and apply it! I scraped up all the money I could find and started taking courses on selling, personal development, marketing and goal setting. My office was great at bringing learning opportunities to us. (Thank you, Realty World Richmond!)

I had dipped my toe in the water, and now I was up to my ankles. There was no turning back.

As it turned out, I had chosen the best of times and the worst of times to start a real estate career.

The worst-of-times part was that mortgage interest rates were just under 20%. Prices were dropping like a rock, and the numbers of sales were dropping along with them. It was hard for buyers to get a mortgage from banks, so that's when I learned about creative financing: second mortgages, vendor financing, wrap-arounds and agreements for sale. It was brutal in 1984 for most of the year.

The best-of-times part? It was a full-on "trial by fire." I had to develop resilience, patience, faith and one hell of a reality base. I had to cope with disappointment, frustration, discouragement and doubt, and along with that I had to build an unshakable belief in myself. I was also starting to learn about the cycles of business. The mantra is always "this too shall pass," and that applies to the good times as well as the not so good. And I learned that attitude is everything. Period.

Right before I got my real estate license, I had run my second marathon of 26 miles and 285 yards. The base training was running twenty miles a week for a year followed by the *real* training, and the running of two marathons required a three- to four-year commitment. That journey proved to me that the seemingly impossible is indeed possible with five elements: time, consistency, commitment, attention to detail and being coachable. I was learning that real success in anything—including real estate—is indeed a marathon.

So in that climate, I was told to pick a neighbourhood and start a "farm" which is a subdivision or area where a realtor—in my case, a brand new virgin realtor—can hopefully cultivate a future.

It's the concept of sowing and reaping, a favourite Bible story of mine as a child which now became relevant as an adult facing a challenging time. The story involved becoming intimately involved with the cycles of farming: preparing the soil, planting seeds, tending to what was planted and finally, conditions permitting, the magic of a harvest. So I picked out an area in Richmond, BC, known as Montrose Estates—a good middle-class area with an interesting variety of home designs and near schools, parks, shopping, a hospital and the Vancouver International Airport. I originally chose it because I liked the way it all looked and felt to me. It was a neighbourhood I would like to live in.

Starting a real estate farm area is a long-term project, and I tackled it with determination. It all began in March of 1984. The first thing I did was introduce myself to about 250 homeowners. Always an out-of-the-box thinker, I did it with panache and a big splash.

I took a photo of each house and made a calendar for each property for the year ahead with their home as the feature photo on the top. (When it came time to glue the photos onto the calendars, I learned about the dangers of sniffing glue first-hand.)

Then there was the endless door knocking, rain or shine. (I'm sure there were times when someone opened a door to me and wondered if I had ever heard of an umbrella.)

I hired my fifteen-year-old son, Jason, and his buddy to deliver the monthly newsletters which I designed from scratch and had printed. (In those days we didn't have marketing companies like we do now who do it all for you, and I couldn't have afforded it anyway!)

Despite all that, I continued to see other realtors' signs taking root and growing in MY FARM! I was surprised how much it hurt, and I can't tell you how often I felt totally defeated.

It was August…a hot day. I had just finished a round of door knocking. My feet hurt, and I think I had a sunburn. I had delivered one of my newsletters to a grumpy man polishing his car. He had scowled at me and said, "Oh you're the one delivering all this stuff!" He smirked and chuckled, "Don't worry… you'll give up soon, and I won't see you again." Ouch!

I climbed into my sauna, which was in the shape of a small burgundy Oldsmobile Omega with no air conditioning, and felt a lump in my throat. I think you call that hitting bottom. After a sticky drive home, I shuffled into the bedroom and flopped on the bed. (At least the bedspread felt cool.)

There's a country and western song that describes precisely what was happening to me. It says, "I've got tears in my ears from lying on my back crying my eyes out over you-oo." The "you-oo" of course was my so-called farm. I looked at the ceiling and whispered to myself, "Sharon, I promise we're only going to do this for a year. And then we'll quit." You know that old adage: it's always darkest before the dawn. This was one of those moments. Everything was about to change.

One sunny day a couple of weeks later in the fall of 1984, I knocked on a door where I had faithfully left my marketing stuff for months, and Mary Elias answered the door. My life changed that day.

Mary was a petite, charming woman, and I am forever in her debt. She told me that they had tried to sell about a year ago but couldn't get an offer. She invited me in to have a look and see what I thought.

I couldn't believe my ears. Of course I would love to! I stepped into the foyer and right away I knew one thing I could tell them: they needed a brighter light bulb. Coming in from bright sunlight into a dimly lit foyer was one issue right away—night blindness for the first impression. I told her that, and she said, "Oh what a good idea!" Now I was on a roll. I suggested they change quite a few light bulbs as we went through the home. Then came the back yard. It was paradise, or at least a version of it! There was a Hawaiian-esque detached building with a full-size swimming pool, palm trees, and a bamboo bar with bar stools. I was speechless!

She asked me if I would like to help them sell. I was over the moon! I raced back to the office, did my research, got the paperwork together and met with Mary and her hubby, Peter, that evening. OMG, my very first listing!

I started doing open houses there every Sunday. One significant Sunday, neighbours came by and asked me if I would have time to stop by their house after my open house because they also wanted to sell. I did, and they did, and now I had two listings in the same block in my very own farm. It only took about six months.

Meet Carl and Maggie

The following Sunday during my open house, Carl arrived in my life. He came through the house, we chatted a bit and he left. The next day I got a call from him.

"Remember me? I came through your open house yesterday?"

"Yes of course. Hi Carl."

"Well I went to lots of open houses over the weekend looking for a realtor, and I want you to help us find a house."

OMG, my first buyer! "Of course I'll help you. Tell me all about it. What's your situation, and what do you need?"

Carl and his adorable wife, Maggie, became my first ever buyers. They were moving from Ontario where they had a charming, newer home that they were selling for $95,000. In the Vancouver area, namely Richmond, a similar home was selling for around $150,000 which was well out of their price range.

Managing expectations became the issue. Maggie was in for a big shock. She and I drove around for a couple of weeks looking at the older homes needing renovations. Carl came and went as his work and duties in Ontario dictated and as they were juggling school and daycare for three little ones back "home." I quickly learned that a box of Kleenex can be an important piece of equipment in such circumstances. There were tears. I told Maggie that every house we saw was either a "no" or a "maybe." The "maybe" list was very short.

We did have a few laughs along the way. She had asked me to never show her a house with green shag carpets. But I couldn't help it because in those older homes there was an abundance of shag carpets. When we finally had to take a hard look at our "maybe" list, there were only three houses on it. One of them had green shag carpet, but it was the best of the three overall.

We went back for the third and final visit to survey the less-than-perfect situation. Maggie sighed as she turned to me and whispered, "The carpet…I think it's actually grown since the first time we were here." We couldn't stop giggling. We had become fast friends.

As Maggie was considering a possible offer—knowing it likely wasn't going to get any better—I suddenly had a hunch. I decided to take a peek at what was under the offending greenery. I pulled out an air vent cover and lifted the "grass," and to my absolute delight and amazement, I saw what saved the day—a beautiful hardwood floor! My heart swelled. I knew there was no money for new floors. I checked the other rooms. All hardwood. I told Maggie. It was a goose-bump moment, and the search was over.

They paid $110,000. Today, in 2022, that big lot alone would be worth about a million dollars.

They bought the house, and every time I went there I thanked those floors for making my clients happy and comfortable in a challenging time in their lives.

LIFE LESSON: Always check out your hunches.

When they had Al and me to dinner—visiting a client in their new home was another first for me—the place looked wonderful. Maggie was a real homemaker! After dinner I told them that I had a confession to make. "When you guys asked me to help you when you bought this home, you were my first ever buyers." Surprised silence.

Then Carl brought forth his cheeky, irreverent sense of humour and said, "Oh, so that explains it! I always figured you didn't know what you were doing!"

Another silence, followed by gales of laughter and another glass of the champagne we had brought for the occasion.

I now considered myself a real realtor. I paid some dues, survived adversity, got over myself, had some success and knew that this was definitely for me.

Little did I know what was coming.

2

A Little Knowledge…Can Be a Giant Pain

*"It ain't what you don't know that gets you into trouble. It's
what you know for sure that just ain't so."*
Mark Twain

So now you have a little insight to help with your thoughts about taking the leap and becoming a realtor. Or perhaps you are already a realtor somewhere along the path, wondering if you should have leapt. Or maybe you have been a realtor for some time, wondering if you should keep on leaping. If you aren't a realtor and have no intention of being one, you may be wondering why anyone would! Take the leap, that is.

When you really think about it, you have to ask why anyone would consider such a career. Let's see now…first you cough up several thousand dollars and give yourself a giant headache studying for hours on end doing a university business course. You then subject yourself to the stress of an exam, more mandatory classes and the beginning of monthly fees at your brokerage, after which you start searching for folks who want to sell, hoping they will pick you. (With so many other realtors around, you need a kick-ass presentation. But that's another story.)

Let's say you get a listing. Yippee! Let's hope it's priced well enough to actually sell. Or what if it doesn't sell?

Here's the thing, we realtors only get paid when everybody's happy. We spend our own money up front for the marketing and promotion of our listing. Really? So, wait a minute, if the property never sells, the seller never gets a bill from us? Yes, that is the fact of the matter.

So, what exactly are these expenses to list and market a property?

- Fees to your real estate board that allow you access to market data, statistics, documents and official and required forms. It also gives you access to the online systems and software to prepare contracts and documentation in a professional manner.
- Fees to the multiple listing service, known as MLS, which allows realtors to have access to each other's listings. This increases the exposure of homes for sale and therefore helps realtors to be more effective in matching up buyers with the right home.
- Costs to produce professional photos, floor plans, virtual tours and videos if appropriate.
- Costs for signage and sign service.
- Fees for title searches.
- Fees for strata properties: strata documents from the management company, including strata plans, financial statements, two years of minutes from all meetings, engineering and depreciation reports, and more.

THE LESSON: Be careful what you list and be aware of its "saleability."

It is a big surprise to many fledgling realtors when they discover the real facts. Yes boys and girls, you have to talk to people. You have to put yourself out there. You are basically on your own. Now granted, some people come into real estate with a readymade source of business. For example, members of their family are builders or land developers (and in those cases, intentionally having a family member get a real estate licence is a business strategy). Some realtors go to work for a developer selling new products under construction or not even started yet, also known as "pre-sales." That is indeed having a job: a boss, a set schedule…the usual J-O-B. But I'm talking to the rest of you—to the rest of us—who start with no connections, no experience and, as in my case, not even knowing the neighbourhood or the streets. (And back in the good ol' days, there was no GPS, Google Maps or Google Earth. I had a map book and a sense of adventure to boldly go into cul-de-sacs by mistake and tell people I was just showing them the neighbourhood. Oops!)

So, back to being careful what you commit to as a listing agent. In the words of Kenny Rogers, *"Ya gotta know when to hold 'em and know when to fold 'em!"*

Meet the Real Estate Know-It-All

Many years ago in the late 1990s, a man called me about listing his house. He had seen my signs around, and one near him had a 'Sold' sign on it.

When I arrived, I couldn't help noticing that it was on a very busy four-lane street. Strike one. It was also in need of a junk removal service and a good lawn mower (or a couple of hungry goats). Strike two.

I knocked on the door and a scruffy, unshaven man appeared. His wife was timidly cowering in the background.

He showed me around. It was a clean house but very worn and tired. In fact, it was so worn and tired that it looked dirty. The house didn't smell that great either. Everything sagged including the furniture and even my optimism. (Obviously someone wasn't easily separated from their cash.) Strike three.

We sat down at the kitchen table. I pulled my research out of my briefcase and started my kick-ass presentation. I could see that he was quickly losing interest, so I put that away and pulled out my CMA (Comparative Market Analysis) showing the latest real estate statistics and likely sale price for his house based on recent sales of similar properties. Once he saw the numbers, he stopped me.

"I don't care about all that stuff. I know exactly how to sell my house. I know the secret to selling houses." (This was my first experience with this kind of real estate know-it-all. But certainly not the last.)

I took a deep breath and dared to say, "Oh, ok, you should have told me you're a realtor."

He frowned, "I'm not a realtor."

"Then you're a marketing expert?" (Pure cheek!)

"No."

"Ok, so what is the secret, and how do you know it?"

"The secret is greedy realtors."

"Oh, how does that work?"

"You offer them lots of money, and they get you a big price."

I was sorry I hadn't worn my running shoes. I was already planning an escape route.

"What do you mean a big price?"

"I want to list my house for $50,000 above what you are telling me and offer the buyer's realtor a $10,000 bonus. They will get me the money."

"I see. So offering a $10,000 bonus will increase the market value of your house by $50,000?"

He smirked and nodded. His silent wife never took her eyes off her knees.

"What if it doesn't work?"

"Well, then I won't sell."

Hmmm! My very first run in with a species that was new to me—the real estate know-it-all. It clearly was time to fold 'em.

I started putting my paperwork back in my briefcase. I knew there was no way on earth to reason with him by pointing out all the checks and balances that would prevent his scheme from working. There is no point in sharing facts with anyone whose mind is already made up.

I felt sorry for his wife. I was pretty sure I saw a tear. I knew I couldn't help them. But then I relented a bit as I closed my briefcase and prepared to leave.

"I'm sure you realize that your buyer is likely to need a mortgage. Anyone with enough cash to pay your price can get a much better deal somewhere else. Anyone needing a mortgage will go to a bank or lender, and that means a bank appraiser will review your property and report its value to the bank. The number he will report back to the bank is the one I showed you, $105,000 not $155,000. It's not possible. The only way I will let you list with me is if I have the listing for five years. Maybe prices will go up that much by then."

He stared at me. At least I had shut him up.

"Thanks anyway for having me over to consult with you. I can't help you, but I wish you well." I wanted to say, "Why don't you buy your wife a decent house to live in?" but we never burn bridges. He wanted to look smart and clever and like he knew it all. I heard a sob as I closed the door and took a breath of welcomed fresh air.

If I had thought I could work with him (she had no say whatever), I might have taken the listing but only if I could bring his expectations into line, set up a schedule of market updates and price reductions, and have the listing for a year. However, there was no glimmer of wiggle room. But that's not always so.

Take the case of the Burgundy Bathroom. This was a case where I could actually work with a real estate know-it-all.

Meet Trish and Kevin

Trish and Kevin were a nice couple who had been seeing my ads and signs around, so they called me to have a look at their condo. They already owned a house in a nearby subdivision that they wanted to move into, so it was time to sell their condo. It was in a charming three-story building in an urban neighbourhood, and they had a prime unit on a top floor corner with northeast exposure. (A top floor condo unit can be very hot in the summer, so that particular exposure limits the sun's direct heat.) It was a truly delightful home: spacious, nice layout, lots of windows bringing the outdoors in, and a view of the sky, trees and gardens below. It even had a real kitchen with an eating area opening onto a private balcony through French doors. And a window over the kitchen sink—always a perk! The space was done in gray tones with warm accents including oriental rugs, throw cushions in rich tones and abstract art which was chosen to enhance the design and colour scheme. It was totally orchestrated and show-home ready. I was in heaven, and the angels were singing!

I was delighted to see such a fine display of taste; not really homey but a real show home that would help any buyer see the possibilities. I measured rooms, took notes and loved every minute of it. Trish and Kevin told me all about how they had worked with the developer (they had bought brand new and had some customizing done). It all seemed perfect.

Then we came to the ensuite bathroom. It was stunning but not in any way you're thinking. It was an overly large room (wasted space in my books) with black tile floors and walls, and the room contained a huge corner whirlpool tub, pedestal sink, toilet and bidet which were all in the most intense dark burgundy colour with the shiniest finish I had ever seen. Then came the gold taps.

I felt I had walked into an alternate universe. It was actually shocking. I couldn't tell if this was inspired by Austin Powers' decorator or a high-end bordello. My dreams of the perfect listing were dashed on the rocks of questionable taste.

Now here's the thing, there are two types of decorating. There is "safe decorating" which means easy to move into and live, and you can sell in thirty days if you have to. And then there's "dangerous decorating." This bathroom was dangerous decorating on steroids!

I looked at these two seemingly conservative citizens as my mind grappled with scenes of middle-aged bathtub joys in this unromantic atmosphere of harshness and—get ready for it—super bright pot lights. How unflattering to get naked! Oh and I forgot to mention the mirrors—they could have at least put in the ones they have on cruise ships that make you looked tanned with ten years less exposure to gravity! And not a dimmer switch in sight, cringe!

Anyway, I listed the property. It was hard to price under the circumstances, and I suggested listing in the $320,000s. Eventually I agreed to a starting-out price of $339,900. I told them the ensuite bathroom could be a problem since it really didn't "flow" with the rest of the condo's lovely traditional decor (a polite way of saying "What the hell happened?") and that someone may want to redo it. I knew it would cost a bundle as I could not see how to get that giant tub out of there without cutting a hole in the roof and bringing in a giant crane or cutting it up in little pieces. I knew the price was too high, but I also knew they were sincere about selling. I explained to them that we may need to adjust the price, and I believed we could work together. So far so good.

So, now, when a potential buyer saw the ensuite bathroom, they either had to:

a. love it,
b. be visually challenged,

c.   be looking for a location to shoot kinky porn,

d.   be willing to pay to redo the room, or

e.   choose none of the above

One hundred percent we were choosing "e."

A month or so went by and we had lots of showings but no offers. Feedback told me the problem was the ensuite: too much work, hassle and money.

I made an appointment to discuss the matter. We decided to reduce the price $5,000 to $334,900. Kevin wouldn't go any lower, although I suggested it. He told me, "That's it. I'm not coming down any lower. I'm not giving it away."

"Kevin, I hear you loud and clear. We will leave it at that price and hope for the best." As I left with a price reduction in hand, Trish rolled her eyes at me, and that said it all.

As is normal, after about thirty days, showings pretty well dried up. We had a showing about every ten days over the next two months. It was dismal.

I was driving between appointments when my car phone rang. It was Kevin. He was speaking loudly. Well, shouting, actually.

"Sharon, we need to talk!"

"Hi Kevin, how's it going?"

"Not good. I'm not happy."

"Ok, tell me about it."

"I want my place sold, and I've had enough of this!"

"Ya know, Kevin, I was just thinking the same. I've had enough of this too."

Silence.

"I've given you my best advice and expertise, spent my time and money, and I've had enough too!"

More surprised silence. A throat being cleared. "Well, what do you suggest?"

"Kevin, I've already suggested it. Your price is too high. We can either get your price to a place where someone will make an offer, or we can cancel the listing. Your call. Either is fine with me."

"Ok, well, Trish wants to drop the price, so let's try that." (Notice it was not *him*.)

We met that evening and dropped the price to $319,900. We had an offer in a week, and it sold for $315,000.

Kevin was a real estate know-it-all. He was also stubborn and wanted to be right. But he was a good guy in the end. (And hey, we all love to be right.)

These were two cases where I fortunately made the right choices. I wasn't going to work for nothing and spend my money until a pay-day came…if it ever did. Learning when to walk away is a major skill for this sort of an entrepreneur.

THE LESSON: Whenever possible, give your time and energy only to the worthy and the reasonable.

Let's stop there for a minute and ask a darn-good question: what is an entrepreneur anyway?

A dictionary says this:

en·tre·pre·neur
noun
1. a person who organizes and operates a business or businesses, taking on greater than normal financial risks in order to do so.

Jack Canfield (a major guru in my life) says that, as a rule, entre-preneurs show signs of this trait early in life. This condition showed up in me in what I call "creative bossiness." Folks who know me will likely tell you that it has not gone away. As a professional entrepre-neur, I now dare to call it (and pray that it is) leadership.

My first memory of this motivated state showing up was in the area of entertainment; getting friends together and directing plays for our parents, I had no trouble getting the kids to do things. One Christmas I was directing a play about Rudolph the Red-Nosed Reindeer. My friend Wendy was to be Rudolph. In her yard there was an adorable little forest with small evergreen trees that just happened to be sprinkled with snow. I was my own locations expert, and this was perfect. The parents would have to stand on one side of the "stage," hugging themselves as they shivered (a common parental state for all kinds of winter events). I was about nine, and Wendy was seven and very cute. I pinned her little brown mittens to the top of her head like little floppy ears and painted her little nose red with my mom's lipstick. (Turned out it was indelible, and her little nose was pink for a week much to the consternation of her mom. Another oops.) But the play got good reviews from the three people who had to watch it. We were a hit.

Then there was my backyard circus period. This time we had five people attending, and they even had to pay. My friend Doris was the fortune teller, and another kid was dressed up as a clown (she could do cartwheels and summersaults and that was about it). My dog and I were the major headliner. My mom had taught Boots, our sweet black cocker spaniel, many tricks and that was what made the day. (That, and we sold homemade cookies.)

I made $2.94, and I took it on the bus downtown to the radio station in Victoria (BC, Canada) and donated it to the Orphans Fund as per Uncle Ed's kiddies' show that was on every weekday at four o'clock. I never missed it, and Uncle Ed was always advertising to donate to the orphans. So, I did.

Nowadays it's all about the food bank for me. Giving back is a must-do for everyone, even if it's not a lot. Many years ago, I took my young children with me canvassing for the Cancer Society. We knocked on doors asking for donations. The kids were amazed at how many people said no. Many folks in big houses with two or more cars said no. Many said they gave at the office. (I hoped it was true.) Then we came to a little run-down house. Someone had made it look pretty with a few flowers at the front door. An elderly lady came to the door and donated a quarter with an apology.

"Sorry, it's all I can spare," she said with an embarrassed smile as she hugged her worn gray cardigan around her tiny body.

"Thank you so much," I said. "If everyone in Canada gave a quarter, we would have millions."

She said, "Thank you for doing this." And we carried on.

My son and daughter found that amazing. They were around five and six years old at the time.

LIFE LESSON: Always give what you can. Grab one of those "$2 for the food bank" slips at the checkout of your food market. Your two dollars becomes six dollars in the hands of the food bank, so it's a smart financial move! My theory is you can't do anything if you're hungry. (If I make any money from this book, a bunch of it will go to the food bank.)

Now back to entrepreneurship and the topic of leadership.

In business, as in life, there are various definitions of leadership depending on your life experience and frame of reference. Let's call them the "intentional leader" and the "accidental leader."

The intentional leader is often a very smart person who sets an intention to get somewhere (for example: to be the CEO of a major corporation or head of an organization), sometimes known as the boss.

(Side note: I see this trend changing, thank goodness. Things are more team oriented with more employee-centred workplaces that are creating willingness to follow and be a part of the whole process—not so much the old authoritarian top-down style—and it's about time!)

The accidental leader is generally more powerful than any elected official. Some may call it "leading from behind." (Examples are Dr.

Martin Luther King, Mother Teresa, Mahatma Ghandi, Nelson Mandela, Oprah Winfrey, Marianne Williamson, Jack Canfield, Jesus Christ, Buddha, Mohammed and more.) This type of leader has inspired more people than many a CEO or political "leader." Following their ideas and example is totally voluntary. (Of course there are always exceptions.) People choose to follow these leaders who tend to rise up from obscurity to support a cause and shine a light in a place of darkness. Folks start following their influence because of their authenticity and courage. They offer hope as well as something bigger to believe in, and they are shining examples of what a difference anyone could make.

So now coming back to earth and to being a realtor, as a realtor you want to lead people in a special way. You lead them to the right process and the necessary knowledge they need to be empowered in the decisions they are going to make. People are hungry for someone to take the lead, show them the right steps in the right order, and assure them that "we got this." When clients choose to follow your lead, it is completely voluntary. They can go with any realtor, and there are lots of good realtors out there.

How do we do that? Simple. We care more.

We care about them, their circumstances and their outcomes more than anyone else. It's all about them, and we have no agenda other than theirs. There's a name for this and it's called "pure intention." I heard this phrase many years ago when I took a workshop with Danielle Kennedy. She is an American real estate legend. (Check out her books, especially *Super Natural Selling for Everyday People*.) Pure intention is defined as the sincere and selfless desire to be of service with no ulterior motive, to say what you really mean and mean what you say, to have impeccable integrity and to treat your client's intentions as if they were yours.

Here's an example of the opposite. I used to work with a realtor who never heard of pure intention and may not have been able to understand it anyway. I accidentally overheard him talking with his assistant. (She hadn't been with him long and didn't stay long either. No kidding!)

"You know that house you sold to Mrs. Jackson? It's all wrong for her," she said.

"Yeah, I know. She'll live there for a year or so, and then we'll sell her out of that house and sell her into a different house. I can use the money!"

This guy was a top producer who certainly didn't need the money, and he was one of those guys who could talk almost anyone into almost anything. Obviously, he talked Mrs. Jackson into this particular mistake that would end up costing her thousands (which would end up in his bank account). I hate to see vulnerable people getting taken advantage of like that.

LIFE LESSON: The best way to lead is by example. Listen well, ask good questions, teach good lessons and be present.

For now, let`s head to the seaside.

3

Life Is a Beach...Or Is It?
Picking Your Battles

*"Never give up because you never
know what the tide will bring in the next day."*
Tom Hanks

So first you dipped your toe in. Then you got your feet wet. Then you were up to your ankles. And now the question appears: how deep will you decide wade in; how deep will you go?

Just like when we were kids and went to swimming lessons, we first learned to float. We learned to kick and paddle and use our arms and, finally, to actually swim. We had to overcome fear of the water and, in fact, make friends with it. Water, a beautiful gift or a deadly enemy?

The question is, will you decide to sink or swim? It's pretty much one or the other.

Let's carry on with this analogy. How far do you want to swim? The width? The length? A hundred lengths? Don't panic; it takes time to decide how far you want to swim.

When it comes to success, including in real estate, it depends how far you want to swim or how high you want to fly. (*Jonathan Livingston Seagull* was a trendy book about that very topic back in the day. It's still a good short read.)

If a person decides to "go all the way" (not the same meaning back in the 1950s when I was growing up and that was something we weren't supposed to do!) it's gonna take some jam (also known as guts, balls, or whatever you wanna call that extraordinary resilience that makes people decide to reject the mediocrity of the world). Nobody ever had any level of great success without sacrifice and effort. It's called work and personal growth. It also takes time and patience—patience with ourselves and others. And elements of character. (More on that later.)

Oh, one more thing…love.

My first year in real estate, I had a lot to learn. I was out on a limb and knew it. I did open houses by the score; two every Saturday and two every Sunday for other realtors' listings. It was spring and summer by then and light later in the day. I held the open houses from 2 p.m. to 4 p.m. and 4:30 p.m. to 6:30 p.m. at two different houses. When it was dead quiet (meaning no one coming into my open house), I borrowed the seller's phone to make cold calls (everyone had a land line back then, and local calls were free). In those days we had lists of addresses and phone numbers for entire municipalities. It was fascinating. Some people hung up on me. Some just wanted to talk and I could not get off the phone. But I got good at it. Now I was getting in up to my knees.

Meet Dave and Betty

One significant day, I made a decision to make a hundred and fifty cold calls in one week. Imagine that! A daunting goal, and I did it.

One of those calls led me to eleven sales over a period of years. Yes, eleven! I made contact with Dave and Betty, and a hard lesson was about to enter my world that would also be a rewarding journey I could have never anticipated. It was 1986, two years into my career.

(Ring…ring…)

"Hello." (It was Dave.)

"Hello, this is Sharon Mason calling. I'm a realtor with Realty World. First may I ask you if I've caught you at a good time or a bad time? Have you got a couple of minutes?"

"Sure, I guess so."

"I'm doing some work in and around your area and wondering if I may be of service to you. Are you curious about home sale prices or maybe considering a move?"

"Well, actually, we are planning on selling."

"May I ask where you are in that process?"

"Just thinking about it really, but we could move any time."

"Oh, ok. What I could offer to do for you is familiarize myself with your home, take some measurements, and do some research for you. Then I could come back with data on the value of your property, what other owners are listing for and, more importantly, what they are selling for. Would that be helpful?"

"That would be very helpful."

"Happy to do that for you. I like to do an evaluation of a property in two steps, if that's ok. First I view the property, and then I come back with the results."

"Sure, that sounds good."

"If you sell, do you have an idea where you might move to?"

"Not really. We'll be staying in Richmond. We just want something different and newer."

"Ok we can talk about that too. When might it work for my first visit?"

"My wife is out right now but we're pretty flexible. She should be home soon."

"Why don't you check with her and let me know. Shall I check in with you this evening or tomorrow?"

"This evening is good."

"Alright then, I'll give you a call around 7:30. Is that ok?"

"Yup, that's good."

"Thanks for taking the time to chat. I really appreciate it."

"I'm glad you called."

The beginning of a beautiful friendship.

The minute I walked into their home with my measuring tape and notepad, it just felt easy. After they showed me around and we measured the rooms and outside dimensions of the house, we sat down in the kitchen for tea. We started sharing information about ourselves, and the conversation led to our pets. That is always a bonding experience. We ended up talking about how hard it is when it's their time to pass on. We told funny stories about their furry lives. We all teared up a couple of times. They were lovely kind-hearted people, probably forty-ish, no kids, hardworking and honest to the point of bluntness (just what I like in people; it makes life easy).

I listed their property, and it went public in the multiple listing service catalogue. In those days we had a book of listings, one per area, printed once a week, arranged by categories (detached houses, townhouses and apartments) and also by price (lowest to highest). I had researched and double-checked all my information. Listings have to be accurate, including square footage of the house, room sizes, age, lot size, property taxes, etc.

It felt good to see my sign on the front lawn. An older base-ment-entry, two-level "BC box" as we used to call them. Nothing special but clean and saleable. The big attraction was the large corner lot where someone could eventually tear down and build a gorgeous new home. A realtor brought us an offer from a family who planned to do just that.

Meanwhile, Dave and Betty and I had been out looking at places they might want to move to. They were fun, practical, outspoken and easy to work with, and we had zeroed in on a few possibilities.

One very busy day a realtor colleague—a lovely man named Ron Dewsbury—called me.

"Hi Sharon, it's Ron."

"Oh yeah, hi Ron."

"I just want to tell you that I think your lot size is wrong in your Lucas Road listing." (My new listing.)

"Oh! Ok thanks Ron, I'll check it out."

"I was looking at the area maps at city hall the other day, and I think you should check it out."

"Thanks so much Ron. I sure will."

I went back to the information I had and recalculated what I was looking at, and it all seemed correct to me. Then I forgot all about it in the busyness of appointments with buyers and my other listings.

I got to know Dave and Betty very well during this two-month period between the offer and the completion date. They purchased a home with me and started packing. When completion day rolled around for the home they were selling, I was in for a nasty surprise.

You probably guessed it already that I did indeed have the lot size wrong. It was quite a bit smaller than I had posted in the listing.

An error like this one has a couple of serious consequences. First, the family who were buying the property wanted to build a new home on this lot. A smaller lot meant they could not build as big a home as they were expecting. That could mean more expenses, redesigning the plans, applying for new permits, inconvenience, complications and disappointment.

The other issue is price per square foot (PPSF). When it comes to land values, the calculation of PPSF is a major factor. They had agreed to pay for a bigger lot than they were getting so, of course, the recalculation would mean a lower purchase price.

The buyers had obviously been making plans and looking at what they could build and had discovered the discrepancy at some point. They hadn't shared the information until closing day when they would have me and my sellers over a barrel, likely on the advice of their lawyer in order to drive the hardest bargain.

I was called to their lawyer's office on completion day. We were all in the office: the lawyer, the buyers (husband and wife) and I. The lawyer told me that the lot size was out, and by how much, and that the buyers still wanted to complete the transaction but that they could not pay the price agreed to in the contract. It turned out they wanted an amount that equalled my share of the real estate fees (about $4,000 plus another $3,000), and the lawyer put it in those exact terms.

The husband turned and looked at me. We made eye contact.

"Sharon, it's too bad this happened. We know it was an honest mistake, and we're not going to sue."

To sue, they would have to prove fraud, but even if they lost the case, it likely would have done so much damage that I may have never recovered (lost reputation, maybe a criminal record if they could have convinced a judge that it was indeed fraud).

There are two ways of getting something wrong, or in legal terms, two types of "misrepresentation" (which is a fancy word for lying). Mine was a case of what is called "innocent misrepresentation" which describes an honest mistake that someone (those buyers) based their decisions on. Then there's "fraudulent misrepresentation" which describes lying for a purpose (like forging someone's name on a cheque or a contract). My mistake was totally innocent; I was in no way trying to defraud.

I was grateful for their offer. They could have asked for a lot more, like a bigger amount of money and possibly my real estate licence. I had messed up, and they had a right to pay less for the property. My best strategy was to forego my real estate fee of $4,000 and deal with the other $3,000 as best I could.

Dave and Betty's purchase was closing the next day. Ouch! Blessedly this would not affect their purchase. They would still have enough money to complete on their new home. I knew I was getting off easy and was happy to forego my realtor fee. But my clients were out $3,000. I had let them down. There were tears (mine).

I had to face the music. I went straight to their house.

When I knocked on their door, they already knew what happened from their lawyer who was representing them in their sale as well as their purchase. Fortunately, they were both home. No one was smiling. We sat down.

We looked at each other, and I plunged ahead.

"I owe you guys $3,000, and I'm going to make it up to you. I can give you $500 a month for the next six months. If I can pay it back faster, I will. I hope that's ok."

Betty pursed her lips. Uh-oh! They could report me to the real estate board...or worse. I threw myself on their mercy.

She spoke, "Well Sharon, our friends all said we should sue you, and we told them we didn't want to do that. Everybody makes mistakes. The $500 a month is fine."

The first of the month was two weeks away. I was at their door that day and the first of each and every month for the next five. When I had made the last payment, we were at their new kitchen table in their new kitchen once again having tea. Dave smiled gently.

"Our friends all said you would never pay back the money like you promised. We told them you would. It's nice to be right, and thank you." I was eternally grateful to these fine understanding humans. I was truly blessed, and I knew it.

Today in the 2020s, things are different. First of all, no more catalogues. Those books had tiny black and white photos of the front of the house and then the basic details (lot size, house size, rooms and sizes, property taxes, and listing realtor information). I recall ten to a page. A far cry from today when we have everything available online and companies selling us services that cover us in many areas. There are companies who do floor plans with all the dimension of the living area and room sizes. Municipalities and cities have websites where you print off surveyed areas and include them online in your listings. We can order a site survey online that will plainly show you the lot dimensions and where any structures are positioned. We publish full colour photos of our properties including interiors, exteriors, neighbourhood features and more. Much, much more convenient. In fact, my real estate board has a rule that realtors must divulge to other realtors where they got their measurements from. And it is customary for us to include a waiver that declares the buyer or buyer's agent should verify everything if important.

But never mind. No matter how much "progress" there is in technology, you can still make a mistake, and a judge will side with a member of the public in most cases. It was then and it is now a face-to-face, belly-to-belly business that is all about relationships and trust.

LIFE LESSON: Be careful and always CYA (short for cover your "tush")!

Over the following decade I helped Dave and Betty move several times and also to purchase some rental condos. Eleven transactions altogether. The bond of trust was so strong, as it is with my long-time clients; they would never consider another realtor. And that's who I want to be—their realtor for life.

Earlier I mentioned elements of character. This situation with Dave and Betty was one example of the tests that come along in any human life. It's about how we handle situations when we wish a giant hole would open up and swallow us; when you hope you can wake up from a seeming nightmare or you just want to disappear or run away. These are tests of character and, at the same time, character builders. One just has to tell the truth, do one's best, survive and move on.

LIFE LESSON: When you screw up, take full responsibility, and face the music.

Meet Ben and Susan

The home I helped them sell was a real treat because of the fabulous ocean view with spectacular snow-covered peaks that grace so much of the Pacific Northwest of British Columbia.

When their home went on the market we had tons of activity, and it sold quickly. But before that sale happened, I had a call from Ben. He was ticked off for sure!

"Sharon I am really not happy!"

"Oh Ben, what happened?"

"You don't have enough information on my house on your website!"

"Ben, I am so happy you called. Let's deal with this."

"How's a buyer going to know anything about it? They'll drive around and see the sign and go to your website. It doesn't say much."

"Ben, that's not what people do these days to locate houses that are for sale."

"What do they do? That's what I do!"

"These days they go to their computer or smartphone and put in their wishes, and the device spits out a ton of places with all the data and photos too. And they usually call their realtor who sets up a search of homes, and the clients receive all the new listings."

"I don't know anything about that. I'm not happy!"

Not happy? He was getting angrier! This required emergency tactics.

"Where are you, Ben? Are you available and can we meet somewhere?"

"You want to meet?"

"Yes. I need to resolve this issue with you as soon as possible."

I drove an hour to meet him, and we met on a sunny coffee shop patio. We were both a lot calmer.

Here was the problem. Ben had not been in the market to buy real estate for almost thirty years. During that time, the digital revolution had hit. I was able to explain to him how times had changed and that back in the day there were only two ways to scout houses for sale: driving around to look for signs or looking at newspapers. These methods had been out of date for quite some time.

It was a happy ending, and I learned a good lesson. Nowadays I add a hyperlink to my current listing details on the MLS (multiple listing service) on my website, just in case.

THE LESSON: If someone hasn't bought or sold for five years or more, always treat them like a first-time seller or buyer.

Things are changing so quickly that anything they can remember from last time likely doesn't exist any longer, or it's been changed so as to be unrecognizable. How the public interacts with properties for sale and realtors has undergone a total transformation. Driving around with a notepad and combing through newspapers is a thing of the past. We sit at the computer and Google "houses for sale" and your city, and we are deluged with websites, articles, and all kinds of services—a veritable feast of information without leaving your comfy chair.

Once Ben and I had met over a coffee and had this discussion, all was well. I told Ben that I was pleased we could meet and come to an understanding. He was a lovely man, and I think he appreciated that I ran towards the problem rather than running away from it. And this could not, absolutely not, be done over the phone, or on FaceTime. A very stressful situation for me, but I was determined to take care of my client—my mandate and my promise. It's a muscle that needs to be exercised like anything else, handling a confrontation and then letting it go and getting over it. The home sold quickly and for far more than we expected. Ben and Susan gave my hubby and me a very nice bottle of champagne. It just happened to be our anniversary and the perfect time for a happy ending.

Ben was willing to hear me out but not everyone is like that. (Thank you, Ben.) I have come across the odd person who just wants to be mad and be right. (It's usually a real estate know-it-all.) I try to move away from the situation as best I can and side-step the negativity. Fortunately, most folks respond reasonably to reason, and that is my definition of sanity.

This is the beauty of being a realtor; the parade of humanity walking endlessly through your life. Everyone comes in with their personality, ideas, assumptions, dreams and expectations. The requirement is that of educating, guiding, offering and leading. Another feature of being a realtor for me is a love of not knowing what's coming next. It's never boring. Developing the necessary skills will get you there and allow you to swim a thousand lengths and fly as high as you desire, if you choose. The sense of self-reliance that comes with this growth, this ability to kindly and successfully handle a conflict or a confrontation, is truly wonderful and empowering, but it requires a high degree of self-management and long-term thinking.

Animals, including human beings, possess something called "mirror neurons." These neurons have played a huge part in many survival stories, I am sure. Here's how they work. Let's say someone is angry, telling you off and insulting you (sometimes it's even a family member or co-worker). Our natural tendency is to "mirror" the behavior. It's hardwired. Bar fights are a good example. In the fight-or-flight response, this represents the "fight" reaction. The attack behavior of the other person triggers the attack response behavior in you and reflects it back, thereby retriggering the other person. And so we have an escalating "fight" situation.

It is so tempting to be angry too, to defend oneself with words and behavior that reflect the energy and intention of the "attacker." Situations where it starts with bickering and escalates into a shouting match with insults and slammed doors illustrate this process clearly. So now that we understand that, what do we humans do about it? The skill is not to "bite" (no pun intended); to not play the role.

In my many years of living, I have had many roles including being a counsellor. In that capacity, I have lots of experience dealing with and hearing about the damage done due to out-of-control mirror neurons. Here's my policy on this matter: strike when the iron is cold, whenever possible. Sometimes when our "buttons are pushed" it's not so easy, but it is so worth developing this relationship-saving skill. The heat of the moment is no time to be communicating verbally and especially physically. Once people have cooled off, there is a much better possibility of resolving whatever triggered the situation.

LIFE LESSON: Strike when the iron is cold. Sometimes counting to ten isn't enough.

In any case, it is vitally important to choose your battles…if you can't avoid them.

Meet Mr. Gerard

Mr. Gerard was the executor of an estate along with his sister in Winnipeg. They were referred to me by a realtor colleague. In those days, I was the happy recipient of real estate referrals from all over Canada. My company had an amazing referral network set up all across the continent, and my referral network was strong.

Estate sales are a whole area unto themselves, and they come with a host of issues. I have dealt with estates where the person died with a will in place and also where they had no will. (More on those stories later, but for now here is some background.)

The role of executor, or executrix if it's a female, is as follows. A person, in this case the mother, creates a final will and testament, which is a document that explains how the person wants their assets and possessions distributed after their death. It also sets forth details of who will be in charge of any infant children (kids under the age of majority); who is to become their legal guardian and be responsible for their care, education and so forth. The will may leave certain items to children, grandchildren, friends or whatever their final wishes might be.

The party creating the will is required to name one or more persons as executor. It is the duty of an executor to carry out the wishes of the deceased person and to protect the value of the estate. They have legal status to sell any real estate and manage what is left behind in accordance with the final wishes expressed in the will. The beneficiaries of a will are those individuals who receive monetary or material benefits according what is set forth in the will, often as a result of estate planning, a process that generally requires an estate lawyer to ensure that the will is legal and enforceable in accordance with the laws of the day.

In this case, the mother left a legal and enforceable will and named both her children, Mr. and Miss Gerard, as co-executors. The mother also left them both her house. The property was in my local area, so it was a great fit for me to help them sell.

Here's the thing (a real complication): the son, Mr. Gerard, was living in their mother's house rent free. His motivation to sell could be questioned, though I'm sure he hoped it wouldn't.

I, of course, was working equally for both executors. Their mandate was to make sure their mother's final wishes were carried out. Those wishes, according to the will, were that the house would be sold and the proceeds divided equally between the two kids along with any other assets.

I did my usual two-step listing. I met Mr. Gerard and gathered data about the property, which was a very nice, comfy, welcoming, older, well-maintained home in a good neighbourhood. On my second visit, which brought forth my research on property values, we had to approach the thorny topic of list price (how much to list the house for). In those days, the mid 1990s, I suggested $439,900. Mr. Gerard, as expected, wanted to list much higher. He was talking $499,000. Nope, not if they want to sell!

I told him I would be chatting with his sister in Winnipeg and that they would have to decide together. She, of course, wanted to sell and receive her inheritance.

I met with Miss Gerard over the phone. I had faxed her my research (yes faxed! No email was in sight yet) showing clearly that market value was under $450,000. She knew her "bro" had his own agenda, and it was not popular. She was reasonable. And I was pretty sure that she was paying rent, unlike her brother.

I contacted Mr. Gerard and told him she would not agree to listing at $499,000 and reminded him they would have to come to an agreement. (I would have loved to have been a fly on the wall during that conversation. She was pissed off that he was living free on her inheritance.) Eventually, they agreed to meet in the middle at $469,900. A bit too high but not impossible. The fact was that the house had to be sold and hopefully without someone having to take someone to court.

I have seen too many estate sales and divorces where someone was obstructing the sale and refusing to accept a good market value offer. Finally the other party or parties had to sue the difficult unreasonable party and start a court order process. They hire a lawyer, and if market value and adequate exposure can be proven, the judge will decide in favour of the plaintiff and order the property sold. The problem is that it wastes money. Too often, for the party refusing to sell, it's an issue of getting even or just being downright difficult and stubborn. In this case, Mr. Gerard really loved living there rent free.

Ok, so $469,000. It was such a nice home in such an attractive, older neighbourhood with tree-lined streets and a manicured park with walking trails. We got good offers—better than expected. The highest was $448,000! Sweet!

Mr. Gerard was not impressed. Guess why.

"No way. I'm not giving my mother's house away." (Always a seller's favorite line about "not giving it away.")

"Well, when you get an offer, you always have three choices: accept it, reject it or counter it. I always recommend a counteroffer."

"I'm rejecting it."

"Hmm…I don't know if your sister will agree to that. It is a very good offer."

"I'm not talking to her. The offer is rejected!"

Darn, he seemed like an adult when I first met him.

"Ok, I'll just go then."

And go I did—straight to my phone.

"Hello, it's Sharon. Here's what's happening."

I filled Miss Gerard in on the entire situation and reported the conversation in the kindest way I could.

"Thanks Sharon, leave it with me. We are taking that offer."

I carried on with my day, happy to leave it with her. It was a family matter and out of my jurisdiction.

The next morning, I was on tour with my fellow realtors. We had all just piled out of our cars to view a new office listing when my phone rang. Guess who? Yup, Mr. Gerard, and he had really built up a head of steam.

Remember when I was saying to pick your battles if you can't avoid them? I was about to learn a great lesson, and I joyously pass it onto you.

So back to the story, he was screaming at me (definitely not an adult!).

"Why did you call my sister? I'm the one you're dealing with! You should do what I want! She says she's taking me to court!"

I held the phone out from my ear, and thirty-five realtors were witness to a clear case of spoiled-brat syndrome. More common than you might think. He finally stopped for a breath, and I managed to penetrate the noise. (Somehow I had kept my mirror neurons from kicking in.)

"Mr. Gerard, this is a case where you have to talk to my manager." My manager, Elly, was standing right beside me, and I handed my phone to her.

She calmly took the phone and listened for a few seconds, and then she took the paper our real estate tour addresses were written on and crinkled it up. What was she doing? I was flummoxed. He was still shouting.

When she got a word in edgewise between his shouts and complaints about me, she did something totally amazing.

"I'm having a very hard time hearing you, sir. There's a lot of static on the line." She scrunched up the paper next to the phone and just kept crunching and scrunching, saying the odd words like "sorry" and "words missing" and "can't hear" and "bad connection," and then she hung up. That was that!

I never had to see Mr. Gerard again. We got everything signed by fax (yes, that ancient practice) and I guess he knew he didn't have a leg to stand on. It was the end of his free ride. His sister obviously knew how to handle him and his temper and sense of entitlement.

I've never had to use the crinkled-up paper technique, but I am told that tin foil makes a much more realistic static sound. It was a battle I chose not to fight, and in that moment, I learned that I didn't have to. (Thank you, Elly!)

LIFE LESSON: Always know when to walk away or delegate. (And keep some tin foil handy!)

Let's back up here and look at what realtors do and how it all fits together.

You know the old saying "It takes all kinds to make a world"?

I can't think of another profession where this could be more true. (Maybe a police officer.) As a realtor you deal with every possible type of human interaction. You have your sellers, buyers and their family members and tire-kickers and looky-loos. You also deal with the folks involved in your transactions: other realtors, home inspectors, mortgage brokers and loans officers, appraisers, designers, stagers, lawyers and notaries, your real estate board, the nosy and not-so-nosy neighbours and often an array of kids and pets.

For now, let's focus on the realtors. Here's a scenario: you are a realtor, and you have a buyer you are helping. You may have met them in a variety of ways—maybe at an open house, or at a party or networking group, or perhaps a friend or a referral from a friend. Anyway, you're going to do your best for them. After the preliminaries, which can vary from province to province and state to state, you will have your initial meeting, get any red tape type of paperwork out of the way, set up a game plan and agree on some ground rules. For examples:

"What's your schedule like? When are you available to see property?"

"How do you like to communicate: a call, text or email?"

"How late is too late to call you or text you?"

Then you get down to the nitty gritty. "Do you have a mortgage person, and have you got yourself prequalified for a mortgage?" (The best answer is "I don't need a mortgage. I'm paying cash." But that doesn't happen often enough!)

If the answer is no and no to the above, offer to get them in touch with a trusted mortgage person that you have a stellar relationship with. When you're new, ask your manager or other experienced and sharp realtors for a recommendation. You need someone who knows the ropes and can put deals together for you. Your mortgage guy or gal can make all the difference and can make or break deals. Best practice is to get your peeps working with a "mortgage specialist," who is not necessarily a person sitting in a branch office of a bank. Knowing how to package and present an application is everything. My mortgage guy Sean Chapman—whom I refer to as my "mortgage guru"—has all that down cold. In fact, he shows clients how to improve their chances of getting a mortgage by paying down a car loan or credit card or offering an ex-spouse a lump sum instead of paying an endless stream of alimony. He takes a weak application and makes it a possible dream. That takes years of experience and the wisdom that comes with it. Get a Sean of your own or borrow mine.

Ok, so now you know their price range. You can't start showing property until you know how much they can spend, which equals the mortgage they qualify to borrow plus the cash on hand for a down payment. Now you are ready to start looking for places to show them. I tell my buyer clients two things right away.

1. "I need to take you to view some properties so that I can tune in on what works and what doesn't work for you. This is great for me so that I get you and really understand what we are looking for. Please keep talking to me and tell me exactly what you think of each property."

2. "Buying is more a matter of eliminating than choosing, so get ready because we are going to see the good, the bad, the ugly and the beautiful. You need to see enough of what's wrong to recognize what's right when you see it. You're going to get so much market knowledge in the process that you will be telling me when a place is overpriced or a good deal. And, with every property we see, you will put it into one of two categories: a 'no' or a 'maybe.' And you can always change your mind."

Now you, the realtor, do a search for the size, bedrooms, bathrooms, parking, pets, etc. You will learn how to do that online. It's all there for you, and you set up an ongoing automatic search that will send you and your buyer client all new listings in real time as they come on the market. Yes, I said *real time*. As soon as suitable properties are listed, you both see them. How wonderful the digital age is! The problem is, every other realtor and buyer looking for the same kind of property your buyers want to purchase gets new listings in real time also.

It's time to mention the art of "pouncing." That's when you tell your buyers, "We have to go see this listing NOW or as close to NOW as possible." When that ideal, well-priced listing shows up, you can't wait. We call that a "hot listing," and lots of folks will be showing up for it. This is especially important once your buyers know the market and have seen enough to know the difference.

Meet Leslie

Here is a typical story. My former neighbour and strata council colleague, Leslie Stevenson, called me to sell her condo. (A lovely lady and a favourite neighbour whom I miss dearly.) I had helped Leslie buy this terrific condo three years earlier, and it was still just as terrific. It was a corner unit, all windows and very bright, with two beds, two baths and a great floor plan. She took a few days to get it uncluttered and spotlessly clean, and it went on the market.

The condo market was a little sluggish at the time. Lots of similar condos for sale, so lots of competition. Leslie was smart. We looked at the comparable sales and there was a recent sale of the same basic unit right in her building which sold for $395,000. Bingo! We listed at $399,000. We didn't want to hang around on the market and do price reductions and get stale. The listing went live online for the realtors and the public on a Friday, and on Saturday a wise realtor brought her buyer, an educated buyer, who made an offer immediately of $390,000. Very respectable. We countered the offer at $395,000, and they accepted it, as expected. I knew that the buyer and their realtor were aware of the recent sale of $395,000 which established market value very clearly. Done deal! It was fair to both parties and that's what we like.

During the next few days, I had eighteen calls from other realtors who wanted to show this attractive and well-priced hot listing. "Sorry, already has an offer on it." They didn't pounce. Always remember to pounce when the time is right.

Let's say, for example, you are working with a young couple who are first-time buyers and have a learning curve to go through. They will start out with a wish list, and often it's not within their price range to have everything on that list. There is often a reality check on the horizon, and the realtor's job is to gently help them accept two things.

1. They can't have it all in their price range and will need to decide what they will compromise on.
2. The most important thing is to get into the market. Get on a rung on what is sometimes referred to as the "property ladder." You have to start somewhere. It's not likely to be your absolute dream home, but you can start the climb.

You've been working with these buyers for a while, and they have seen quite a few properties. They saw what sellers were asking and, if you are doing it right, they also have seen what some of those properties sold for. Aha! Market knowledge. Now you can take them to a property and they will say "Wow they are asking too much," or "This place is pretty well priced."

They are now what I call "educated buyers." Once they have accepted the two reality checks above, they are ready to pounce when they see a property they know they can call home. It will likely not be dream-home level, but affordable for them. If it is well priced, clean, well maintained and looks good and new on the market, it's your duty to explain to them that it's going to sell fast.

That is exactly what happened to Leslie. Her buyers saw it on

Friday and bought it on Saturday, day two of being listed. They were ready to pounce before it was gone. (After all their experience and their realtor pointing out the facts of real estate to them, they had a case of FOMO: fear of missing out!)

The sad fact is that a lot of what is on the market is overpriced and doesn't "show well" (realtor talk for "looks good/smells good"). Just take a look at the photos online for some of the properties available. It can be shocking. Your buyers will get to see the difference with your guidance. When you suggest that they might want to make a decision sooner rather than later, they usually hear you loud and clear. If they hesitate and end up competing with other offers, or missing out altogether, then it's often a case of lesson learned. Sometimes they have to learn the hard way; they miss out on the perfect home because they weren't ready to pounce and waited too long to make their offer.

We want our listings to appeal to buyers of course, but our most valuable "clients" are all the other realtors. Let's say there are five thousand realtors in your area, in your real estate board area, and let's say half of them are working with three or so buyers. You can see how many buyers are potentially exposed to your listing by way of your fellow realtors. Some buyers find the listing on their own and call their realtor. Awesome. We always want our listings to shine online through the photos and the write-up. However, there is a special part of a listing that is for the eyes of other realtors only. Make good use of that as well as the public comments. Paint a wonderful word picture of your listing, and make it a work of art.

Here's another thing: You want to be the realtor that other realtors want to deal with. Sorry to say some realtors are cranky, grouchy, uncooperative and therefore unpopular. Always be in service to the other realtor. Our job is to make it so easy for them to sell our listings. Always be building your reputation so that when you pounce with a buyer, the other agent is delighted to be working with a real professional. There will always be issues that come up in any transaction, and the solution-oriented agent is always a treasure to have on board during those times.

Instead of sign and ad calls as in the past, these days I get emails from official real estate websites like realtor.ca. This site has all the multiple listings in Canada. It is the official domain of the real estate industry. Pick your province, your area, price range and everything else you want and set up your search. If a potential client—usually a buyer in, what I call, the kicking-tire stage of moving—sees a property that speaks to them, they can reach out to me for more information. I can offer my services and start a relationship that allows me to help them in their quest. We know that real estate is a hot topic and a bit of a hobby for some folks who can't sleep and love to look at houses. The looky-loos are always with us, and it's not only at open houses but also online which is open all day every day all year! Once in a blue moon do I get a "sign call" now in the digital age. I love those calls. There's a real person there to talk to, and I can visualize them sitting in their car outside my listing talking to me.

THE LESSON: Take every opportunity to educate clients and future clients about the process they are engaged in. Teach them the best ways to navigate the world of buying and selling real estate. Prepare them for what's coming, and that will smooth the way.

Meet Angela and Victor Song

My hubby Al and I were out on a Sunday afternoon scouting townhouses for some clients when we had the happy accident of meeting this charming couple. It was Angela's listing, and they had an open house underway. As Al does for me, Victor accompanied his lovely wife to open houses. It was obvious that they were expecting an addition to their family.

It's good security for us female realtors not to do open houses alone, and buyers often love to talk to a couple. Al and I enjoy taking buyers around together to look at homes. It's fun. Once we have done the grand tour of the property, the guys sometimes go check the guy stuff: garage, furnace, hot water tank, electrical panel, fences, gates and drainage. We women are usually more interested in the kitchen, dining room, primary bedroom, closet space and laundry room. It works out great. Viva la difference!

Anyway, we got chatting with Victor and Angela, and we all totally clicked. Our real estate rules had been changed recently, and Angela and I were discussing the new paperwork we realtors were all busy adapting to. During our conversation I mentioned some new clauses I had learned for listing a property. It was very useful because it made it ok for the listing agent to have a colleague hold an open house at the listed property. Of course, if a realtor has more than one listing that needs to be open, say on a Sunday, it's great to have a colleague who can be at one of them. Good for the seller and good for both realtors too. We had a lovely visit, and I offered to email Angela the clauses I was mentioning. When I got home, I did so. We continued to have a pleasant and informative email exchange.

Angela was a soon-to-be mother, and I was old enough to be her mother for sure. It's always a pleasure to give encouragement to an upcoming real estate superstar, and that is how I saw this kind, funny and caring young woman. Victor and Angela exuded a happy energy that was infectious.

Time passed and one day I received a call from Angela. Their baby daughter had arrived, and she was calling to ask for my help. Little baby Abby was proving to be a full-time job, and Angela was asking me to take over the listing where we had met. She was referring her clients to me. What an honour! It's customary for us realtors to pay a 25% referral fee to the referring agent. I told Angela that I would be delighted to look after her clients, and that she could expect a 25% referral.

"Oh no Sharon! Please don't! I don't want anything."

I was most assuredly right about Angela. Her integrity was over the top. And so was mine.

"Angela, it's my policy that everyone must get paid for their work. If I can't give you a referral fee, I can't take the referral. It's not right, and I could never be comfortable. You have to take it."

"Well, I don't really want to, but I leave that up to you Sharon."

I got that townhouse sold, and Angela got the referral fee. We were all happy. We all had a lovely dinner party just before Christmas: Angela's clients, Victor and Angela, Al and myself and, of course, baby Abby. Like I said, you want to be the realtor that other realtors want to work with.

We are still great friends and good colleagues to this day. When we find good people like Victor and Angela, we never let them go. And I love it when that happens.

Over the years I have known realtors who worked in the business for a while and left the profession for a variety of reasons. Many of these ex-realtors have hired me to list their own homes and get them sold. I always pay the 25% referral too, even though they are no longer realtors. It's always a pleasure! They are easy to work with—not a real estate know-it-all among them—and it's the right thing to do.

I see one of my roles as upholding professional standards and raising the level. I am here to add positivity anywhere I can. I have helped a lot of newer realtors learn some valuable lessons along the way. We are on this earth to help each other, whether it's a client, a fellow realtor, a neighbour or anyone. Always trust the process.

LIFE LESSON: Know that what goes around really does come around. (And sometimes it happens so fast it can make your head spin!) Treat everyone like gold.

4

Getting off the Ground…
Your First Year

"Expect the best,
plan for the worst and prepare to be surprised."
Dennis Waitley

Let's take a look at your first year.

(Confession time: I know absolutely nothing about aeronautics, but I am going to talk about jet planes.)

Starting out in real estate or any business is like getting a jet plane off the ground. I have no idea who came up with this analogy so I can't give credit there, but this concept captures the essence of the topic at hand.

Travelonthefly.com tells us that the average weight of a jet plane is 90,000 pounds when empty (no luggage, no cargo, no fuel or human bodies). Fully loaded you can expect a weight of around

174,000 pounds. Of course this varies with the type of plane, but the idea is consistent. No matter how you slice it, it's one heavy mother. We are going to need enough energy, speed and general oomph to get the aerodynamic principles of flight to kick in. Only then do we experience that magical moment when we are freed from Earth's gravitational pull. Then we soar, often up to thirty-five thousand feet or so. The engines become a secure sounding hum—not the roar of take-off—and it can almost feel like floating, even heaven-like if you're above the clouds.

Now we are going to talk about the business of being a realtor (I do know about that!), specifically the first year of being a realtor. Think of your real estate business as that 174,000-pound monster sitting on the tarmac. How are you going to get it off the ground? That's what we are going to talk about.

One big decision that I hope to help you make is which type of realtor you would like to be? There are two kinds of real estate practices: transactional and relational.

The "transactional" realtor may meet someone at an open house or at a networking event, chat them up, and see if they are in the market to buy or sell. If they are, these realtors offer to help the process along, take them through the steps of their transaction and get paid. Their next contact is when the client's five-year mortgage comes due. The transactional realtor may call them up to see if they want to sell. Or maybe they don't stay in touch at all. Their motivation is to do a deal and get paid.

The "relational" realtor's motivation is to create a relationship for life and earn the loyalty and trust of their clients…AND to get referrals from them. Think about it, which do you think would create a lasting and ongoing source of business and income? Correct! Obviously number two is the right answer. In fact, in my world, it is the only answer.

When you decide to become that long-term asset in your clients' lives, it's a commitment to several things.

First you are building a database. These days it's called the Client Relationship Management system (CRM) and, thank God, it's now digital! In my early years it was simply called a mailing list. It involved designing and printing newsletters and other items and "doing envelopes," which meant writing addresses by hand or on a typewriter (whatever that is) and licking stamps and those yucky envelope flaps. (I finally figured out about a damp sponge.) It's much better nowadays boys and girls! I think I was born too soon.

This precious list IS your business. (No kidding!) Your job is to learn how to attract people to you as their realtor and to be allowed the privilege of having them on your database. Your next job is to make use of that list to make yourself valuable, to serve those folks and to stand out from thousands of other realtors. How do you do this? By being consistent, caring, courteous and a class act. Be different. Be enthusiastic, be energetic and be entertaining. Take some courses or ask your manager and other realtors.

At this point I want to tell you that getting educated in this area is huge. So, here's my take on this topic: The company and the office you choose to go with are important.

There are two major types of offices. Let's go back to the jet-plane idea to talk about them.

1. Flying economy: These companies cost less and, of course, offer less to the realtor. I recently was involved in a transaction where the other realtor had made some serious errors in her contract. She was pretty new in the business, and I didn't have time to train her. (It's not my job anyway.) I have helped many new realtors along the way, so I can tell they are not getting the training and in-house support they seem to need. But in this case, I suggested she call her manager and get some advice and guidance.

    She said, "I can't reach my manager after 5 p.m." It was 9:30

p.m., and my manager was totally available to me. Real estate transactions usually happen after hours or on weekends. Of course they do. That's when many buyers and sellers are not at their day job. That realtor was flying economy. Anyway, I gave her a break and made it ok for her to get the issue fixed. She was doing her best but not getting the help she could have used. This type of situation can be serious and lead to all kinds of trouble. Even with all my experience, I pride myself on being my manager's favourite pest.

2. Flying business class: There's an old saying that is 100% true. You get what you pay for. I encourage everyone around me to think more about value than cost. Real estate companies are no different. You need training, support, encouragement and coaching when you first start out. Go with a company that's going to give you value. You will pay more but you will reap the rewards personally and financially.

   Another factor is that a company with truly professional standards tends to attract and retain professional realtors and often ones with long real estate careers. To be in an environment where there is a wealth of knowledge and experience and people who will share it with you, even partner with you in the early days of your career, and where integrity and hard work are the culture, will nourish your growth in the business. Real estate can be a lonely business, so you want to be part of a culture and of a team with high standards and camaraderie.

So, yes, choosing a good company and office is a very important decision that will help you get your business off the ground and support your ambitions.

Another concept to consider is that of real estate teams. Over time the concept of real estate teams has gained traction. When I was first in the business, most realtors were a one-man band. Frequently two realtors would become real estate partners. We still see that today. Legally they can be considered a team, a team of two.

Before teams became common, we would see a busy realtor hiring an assistant or a buyer's agent. If the lead realtor had a listing, selling that listing would be their main focus. The sellers of that listing, who became buyers, could be passed onto the buyer's agent. The listing agent would be managing all the listing duties: the open houses, taking calls on the property, arranging viewings with other realtors and their buyers, arranging marketing such as photos, feature sheets, staging, cleaning and any repairs needed to get the property ready for viewing. The buyer's agent would take care of the buying end of the business. Even before the listing goes onto the MLS (multiple listing service), the buyer's agent could be showing the clients around to have a look at what's out there so that they have the comfort of some market knowledge and an idea of what they could purchase.

Let's step back and get a broader view of teams. Let's say that there is a top-producing realtor who is selling a lot of real estate, like around fifty-plus deals a year. I know it seems crazy, especially when we are told the average realtor in Canada does three deals a year. Of course, some of those are part-timers—meaning they have another job— but, to me, it's a full-time job, so I don't understand how part time works.

Anyway, I can tell you from experience, that lead realtor is likely heading for burn out. Or worse. This kind of schedule and stress and "no life" can ruin your relationships and your health. A long-time colleague of mine reported the following in a newspaper article: "I gave up my health to make a fortune, and I had to give up my fortune to regain my health." As a Canadian, he had to go to the USA to get the life-saving treatment he needed, and we all know what that costs. (Beaucoup dollars!)

Now that's an extreme case but it is an example of what can happen. Real estate can become an addiction, especially to a driven workaholic. I know about that trap. These days I have a label for myself: recovering workaholic. Finding balance is always critical. More on that later.

Back to the overworked realtor, so she is earning tens of thousands a month. She starts putting a team together. She has two objectives: to lessen the workload and to make the same, or even more, money for herself and therefore her team members.

Here's one possible way she can structure a team situation. She may pay the team member's (herein after referred to as the TM) office expenses and all the team expenses for marketing the listings. The TMs pay for their own business cards, vehicle, phone and the personal stuff. Each is an independent contractor. Then the lead agent provides the TM with clients to work with and, sometimes, jobs to do, like opening up a house for another realtor to show it or putting a "sold" sticker on a for-sale sign. In addition, the TM can find their own leads and clients such as friends and relatives. There are various ways for the TMs to get paid. It depends on the deal the lead agent is offering. If the TM is given a buyer and successfully helps them purchase, the real estate fee may be split 60/40 or 50/50 between the lead agent and the TM, but if the TM brings their own client then there may be a different split. Some teams just split all the income on a percentage basis and work together to make sure everything gets done. There can be many kinds of deals that may be part of how teams are set up to share the workload, responsibilities, expenses and income.

Of course, there are pros and cons to teams. One advantage may be the experience and on-the-job training you could acquire (depends on the team). The team members' costs are minimal, but they have to be helping to bring money and business to the team and freeing up the lead agent to develop more business for the team. With enough help the lead agent can then act like the CEO and be creating more income for everyone. And more work. So it all depends on your personal agenda and what works for you personally.

If you decide to go with a team at any point in your career, make a deal to take any clients you brought to the team with you if you part company in the future. As in everything, you always need a strong exit strategy.

There are big teams and small ones. Some realtors make it a family affair: a mom, a dad, two or three grown kids and maybe their spouses. Or maybe it's a couple, a mother and child, or just two partners. Some teams are huge, like twenty realtors. The entire team writes up all business, listings sold and sales made under the lead agent, and that "lead agent and team" can then be named in the top few for production (numbers of sales and volume of sales) in that real estate board jurisdiction.

It's rare that one person can achieve a hundred or more transactions in a year on their own. The most I ever accomplished in a year is sixty.

If enough business is done, the "Lead Agent" or "Lead Agent and Team" would appear on bus benches or even on sides of busses as "Top 1%" or "Top 10%," whatever the team can achieve in a calendar year. Top 10% is what we call Medallion Club. One person can accomplish that on their own. It's a lot of work and taking of responsibility, and with a loyal database and referrals from friends, family and clients, it is doable. But remember the Canadian average is three transactions a year. Some realtors don't want to merely settle for average. It's the personal growth that will make the difference. (And that topic is coming up soon.)

The big production numbers and awards can attract business, but it can have difficulties as well. I have had feedback from clients who have worked with a team, and they can't get their realtor on the phone when they call with a question or concern. It's not personal enough for them when they are called back by, or have a visit from, a team member. Doing big numbers—being a "Top Producer"—can be a great ego booster, but the service to clients could suffer under the workload. And it takes a lot to sustain over a long period of time. But please be clear, this is not always the case at all.

Here's my take as a realtor dealing with big teams: When my buyer has an issue, I want to speak to the listing agent in person. There have been times when I have only been able to reach a team member who has never seen the property I'm asking about. Just something to be aware of.

For me, being dedicated to the quality of the experience my clients are having is everything. It's my focus. I do my best to take the stress off them by always being available. Sometimes there's a lot of hand holding. (I'm sure I will learn a lot due to the fact that my daughter got her real estate licence while I was writing this book, so I guess I'll have a "team"! She's good at hand holding too!) Buying, selling and moving is an emotional time, and our ability to educate and put out fires—especially before they start—is super important to me.

Some sellers think that if there is a big team they stand a better chance to get more offers from the team, which is not necessarily so. All the members of a team are deemed to be working for the seller, so in my jurisdiction, for example, the team members and listing agent would not be in a position to represent a buyer as well as their seller at the same time. It's a conflict of interest. (More on this topic later.)

In the past I've had a couple of assistants and a partner, and I found, for me (and it's just me), that more people brought more complications. I'm a fan of the KISS theory: keep it simple, Star! And I am one of those people who likes to do my thing my way. I've tried a lot of stuff over the years, and I know what works for me—being consistent and keeping it personal. Your job will be to find what works for you and working in a team could be it!

Being a real estate assistant is another way to go as well. Well established, busy realtors often hire an assistant. In fact, two or more realtors may share an assistant. Many are unlicensed and many assistants are paid a salary. A licensed assistant can do things an unlicensed one cannot, like hold an open house, present an offer for a buyer or seller, give information about a property, show property and more. This can be a fantastic training ground for anyone who wants to jump into the deep end of the pool. I know of many folks who became an unlicensed assistant to see if they should become a realtor. Some do, some don't. Some end up with burn out. I met one realtor recently who was an assistant and got her licence so that she didn't have to work so hard. Go figure!

If you are working for a developer, you are also working in a team. There might be a lead agent or maybe a sales manager, and you have regular hours and usually get paid on results. Everyone generally shares in the fees generated by the overall sales. It can be a commitment of years while a project is under construction, after construction is completed, and while it's selling out. This works for a lot of people.

LIFE LESSON: Take the time to understand what your choices are, and weigh the pros and cons carefully. Get all your questions answered. Listen to your intuition. Reflect and evaluate.

No matter what path you choose, always be aware that training is everything.

As I touched on earlier, in my first year I did indeed seek out every training opportunity I could possibly find. I would be with people, like at an open house for example, and I knew there was something I should be saying to them, but I had no idea what it was. Then someone told me about a trainer named Floyd Wickman. (Back in those days we had cassette tapes. Ever heard of those? Nowadays you can Google Floyd's training and see it all on YouTube.) Floyd saved me. That's when I discovered "scripts"—also known as words that work. Floyd had great scripts that made all the difference to me. At least I had a track to run on. I had words I was memorizing and practicing in front of a mirror, and I recorded my own voice saying those magical phrases.

It's like cooking. First you follow the recipe, then you make it your own. You add a little garlic or soy sauce. You add cream instead of milk. You make it a little Italian with some oregano. You know what I mean. With a script, you learn it word for word. Then over time you make it your own. You get comfortable, and it's a natural flow of thoughts and words that are meant to offer service, truth, competence and willingness to make things easier for the prospective client.

At Realty World where I started out, we had to memorize the Realty World listing presentation. They even had a contest for the best presentation in each class of fledgling realtors. It was a great way to truly help us get some practice. The imaginary sellers were the famous Mr. and Mrs. Jones. (Not the ones we've all been trying to keep up with all these years!)

"Mr. and Mrs. Jones, thank you very much for allowing me to meet with you to discuss the marketing of your home. Before I do that, may I acquaint you with my company Realty World and the services we offer to ensure that you get the best result? [Yes.] Thank you. At Realty World we have a complete marketing system from beginning to end. Nothing is left to chance." And so on. That at least was the gist of the presentation. We also had photo boards and booklets; old school and very effective in the day. Some might also say revolutionary!

We pioneered mall kiosks with displays of properties for sale, manned with real live realtors people could talk to right there in the middle of a busy mall. It was genius! We had these giant property boards with full colour photos and all the details of the property right there for anyone to see. And it was all patented, so other companies couldn't copy us. It gave us that edge in the market place that allowed the company I was with to dominate the area for many years.

Realty World has gone from our area now. They sold to a bigger company in the late 1990s. Currently, my HomeLife office has a big mall display that reflects the trends of the twenty-first century. Our listings are displayed with all details in full colour on big screen TVs and small property boards as well. And it still attracts clients and gives our listings great exposure. Even with all the online shopping, the mall is still a place where people go and hang out.

Over time I made that Mr-and-Mrs-Jones presentation my own. As times changed and as the market fluctuated, I added charts, diagrams, statistics and stories of current real estate situations. Visuals are great, but stories? They are the glue that holds it all together. If a client has questions or concerns, a story relating the experience of another seller or buyer can be a game changer. Realtors collect amazing stories over the years; stories that provide effective teaching opportunities. Tools of the trade. (You might notice quite a few in this book!)

Collect some scripts and start using them with folks you meet who are asking you about real estate. Then start to notice things that you personally come up with, maybe even accidentally! Make those scripts conscious and keep using them. Let your own natural words fall on the right ears. It's magic.

You know how occasionally there is something random that just sticks in your memory crystal clear? Here's one. I found a course I could afford. It was taught by a smart, sincere man, Allan Bayliss, and it cost $400 in 1984. I lot of dough at the time! Anyway, it was my first training. We were in a small conference room in a hotel. There were about eight of us in the class, and one lady there made a huge difference in my life as a realtor. (I can't remember her name, but if she's reading this book, I hope she gets in touch.) At one point in the day, Allan went around the room and asked everyone to share one thing about how they do their business. I, of course, didn't have a business yet, so I just said I was there to listen and learn. He said that I was amazing and would obviously become a superstar because of my attitude. That made me feel good and daringly optimistic too as I continued to step off that cliff.

Then he came to this lady. It was her turn, and I was all ears.

"I've been in real estate for [I think she said] twelve years, and I know that the biggest complaint is that people never hear from their realtor who listed their house unless there's a showing. Well, right now, I have seventeen listings, and I call all my sellers every Friday. I give them a weekly update on the market, on any calls I've had on their property and to see how they are doing. Even if the news I have is not good, I call and tell them what the real deal is. They appreciate it and I feel good that I did it."

You may remember what the market was like when I started out: sky-high interest rates, up near 20%, and house prices falling like a rock. I had so much respect for this lady and her commitment to her clients; she told it like it was! The media was full of the same data, but folks want to hear it from their realtor. It's a matter of respect.

Sometimes I call my clients way more than once a week during a transaction. I can always find an excuse, like "a house on your street was just listed today" or "let's get together for a market update."

I get to be their favourite pest too, not just my manager's. In fact, I regularly identify myself as a favourite pest. Never hurts to add humour to any situation, especially one where I might be actually bugging someone.

So in your first year, get yourself into an environment that will nurture you. Be a sponge and say yes to every opportunity that comes along for learning and experience. Do open houses when possible (sometimes things make that impossible, like the Covid period). Join networking groups, and spread the word online (social media, emails, and texts). Tell everyone you know, and keep letting them know, what you are doing and that you are working with a team of highly experienced realtors, your manager and office colleagues. When you are new, people will see you as inexperienced, so you want to calm that assumption as much as possible. Surround yourself with help if and when you need it, and "boldly go!"

The more you raise your game to project a truly professional image, the better. It's a good idea to send a letter by snail mail. Make a big announcement and include your new business cards. Back it up with an email, and create a snazzy signature for yourself. Use your company logo.

Create a motto. "Your best way home." My company uses this and so do I. I also use "Your family realtor through the generations." (It will take time before you can legitimately steal that one!)

Always include your photo on everything, and don't use your high school photo unless you just graduated. Make it professional and make sure it looks like you.

Put everyone on your database and find a way to keep in touch with them. Let them know what you're doing in real estate. Email and post your first sale, your first listing, or a diploma from a course you took. And get testimonials from your clients. Post them. Toot your own horn. Make it comfortable for you to brag.

Or email a photo of the property with yourself and your clients, and always thank them. Always remind your supporters that you are never too busy for their referrals. Email a "Just listed!" and "Just Sold!" announcement and write, *Thank you Fred and Joan! By the way I'm never too busy for your referrals!*

Keep letting them know you're still in the business. It's called "top of mind" and all companies do it (and if they don't, they should). Who do you think of when you think of office supplies? Staples and Office Depot. DIY home projects? Home Depot. Top of mind is what you want to be to your database and everyone you know.

So now your jet plane should be rolling down the runway, the engines running and revving up. Maybe you're even off the ground, gaining experience and the confidence that comes with it. You know where to find what you need to know, and you have a system in place. Whether you're new or looking for a fresh start, there are some thoughts here that could be useful and effective. Keep reading books on self-development (examples: Jack Canfield, Brian Tracey, and Jim Rohn). It's everything! Keep taking classes, webinars and workshops, and have stellar work habits. Touch your business each and every day and know that people need you. You will attract the right ones if you put yourself out there.

Remember, we realtors help people with the single most important thing in anyone's life: their home. Some people say it's only business, but it cannot be. It's their home, and it's usually the largest single investment in anyone's lifetime. It is major. And they are counting on us—on you—to bring your A-game. And your heart. Love your clients, and cherish the meaningful work you are able to do and the service you are able to give. It's a gift and a privilege.

LIFE LESSONS: Always be coachable. Follow those who have already gone where you want to go. Know your strengths and work on your weaknesses.

5

Estate Sales... Seriously?

"Being of sound mind, I spent all my money."

Anonymous

A discussion around estates and estate sales definitely deserves its own chapter, so here it goes.

Reality check: David Chilton, who wrote the amazing bestseller The Wealthy Barber, points out very bluntly that if you're an adult and you don't have an up-to-date will,"[i]t's ridiculous. It's lazy. It's selfish. It's irresponsible. It's unfair."

He said it, so I don't have to. Thank you, David Chilton!

We know that 60% to 70% of Canadians don't have an up-to-date will or any will at all, and we also know what percentage of us are going to need one. Yes, boys and girls, 100% of us need one. Even if there is a will, the contents may be out of date, illegal by current laws, unwise and even unkind to your loved ones. Proper legal advice from an estate lawyer should not be negotiable.

As a realtor, you will run into situations that involve estates left behind by deceased persons. Your role will involve either representing the estate in listing and selling any real estate property, or you may represent a buyer purchasing a property for sale by an estate and its representatives.

Being involved with an estate sale involves a learning curve for a realtor who is unfamiliar with the process. You do not have to navigate these waters alone. Your manager is there to guide you through. It's a step-by-step process. There will be legal documents required by your real estate board that you will submit with your listing: the will and the documents proving that the executor has the right to dispose of (sell) the real estate asset. You will be dealing with the executor or executors, and you will have your manager to turn to for support. Your real estate board offers courses on specialized areas of knowledge, like estate sales and other areas of required knowledge.

Be prepared for the executors, who represent the estate and the wishes of the deceased, and, in some cases, beneficiaries, who are to receive money and other items from the estate. You often find a minefield of family issues with high emotional content as well as other circumstances and complications that one could never predict. The case of Mr. Gerard most certainly gave us a peek into a scenario like that!

Meet Marcy and Dan

Anita, a dear friend of mine, referred Marcy and Dan to me. Their mom had died, and they needed to sell her condo. Marcy lived in another part of Canada, and Dan was in the southern USA.

Marcy was in town to get the condo ready to sell and wanted to meet me to get the ball rolling. The very attractive two-bed, two-bath condo was in the process of being painted. (That is always a good thing. Realtors commonly refer to paint as "a million dollars in a can.") Anita told me it was pretty cluttered, as many homes of the elderly can be, so I arranged to have my stager, Joanne, give Marcy some advice. I spoke to Marcy, and we met at the condo. There was a lot to do, and there was Marcy, grief stricken as she was, carrying out her mom's wishes. One of those wishes was that both Marcy and Dan be co-executors, meaning that their mandate was to carry out their mom's wishes according to the will. They were also co-beneficiaries, meaning they would split the proceeds equally.

Fortunately and thankfully Mom had a clear and legal will. (What a gift to her kids!) The first step is for a lawyer to take the will through a process called "probate." In probate, the will goes before the court and (hopefully) is declared "approved" which means that the executor(s) are authorized to sell the assets and that the estate has paid a fee to the government.

A property *can* be sold prior to probate being acknowledged by the courts, but ownership and possession of the property cannot take place until after probate. In a case like that, the property is considered sold but everyone has to wait until the courts get to it. As a rule, it's better to wait until probate is granted, and then the transfer of ownership can happen in a normal fashion.

And just for the record, if someone dies without a will, it gets very complicated. If there is no executor, there is no one to take responsibility for disposing of the property and the possessions of the deceased person (or what happens to any minor children for that matter). At that point, the Public Trustee may step in and take care of it all. And they charge fees for doing that; to my knowledge, up to 50% of an estate may go to government agencies. Minor children can end up in the system even if the deceased parent believed that their mom, sister or best friend would take the children. If it's not in writing, it won't happen as a rule. It can all take years and can ruin a family.

Back to Marcy and Dan, their mom's will had gone through probate, meaning that it could now be sold and the title for the property could be transferred to a new owner.

After about three weeks, the condo was market ready. Tons of old, irrelevant paperwork and decades of other saved-just-in-case items had been let go of via donations to charities and lots of recycling. It was painful for Marcy to go through her beloved mom's life and let go. She, of course, kept some treasures for herself and her brother. Professional photos were taken, and all the listing preliminaries were under way.

As you know, the important business of establishing a listing and possible sale price is always a critical step. It's the inevitable CMA: comparative market analysis. As a realtor, I look at recent sales of similar properties: similar size, age, numbers of bedrooms, bathrooms, parking issues, updates, condition of the property, and location. I want to check up on a lot of factors so that I can be fully knowledgeable about the condos I am using to establish a likely value for the seller. It's all online provided by my real estate board and is available to all realtors.

The other way to establish value is by getting an appraisal by a hired certified professional who does it for a living. They use all the same comparables that we realtors do, and many times I have had appraisers call me to ask what I think a property is worth. If you're getting a mortgage, your lender will likely be sending an appraiser to check up on the property and the value of it. It costs a few hundred bucks and it's one of the costs of buying.

As it turned out, the last sale in the building of a similar condo had sold for $305,000. And that was fair market value. Research in other similar condo buildings proved it as well. (Several years ago, around 2014, the condo market in my area was soft. In fact, we had seen condo prices dropping. Of course, they came back with a vengeance years later when detached house prices and even townhouses soared out of the reach of many.)

Marcy, Dan and I met on the phone. I had emailed the comparables to Dan and Marcy so that we could all share the data together. I explained the market conditions, and I showed them all the data regarding expired listings. (Expired listings are places that had not sold because the list price was too high.) We talked about the best strategy for getting an offer in the first three to four weeks when the listing was fresh and getting that big flurry of activity that always happens with a new listing. No amount of price reductions can ever recreate that opportunity. I explained how realtors set up a search and about the pouncing probability by an educated buyer who has seen everything and knows a realistic deal when they see one (like at Leslie's condo).

Marcy was on board with my advice. But Dan, well no way was he listing below $329,900! (Uh-oh, Mr. Know-It-All strikes again. Too bad Marcy wasn't the only executor.) She was adamant that we list at my price of $315,000. Anyway, after a time of the two of them "talking"—Marcy pointing out that they were paying out every month for the monthly maintenance, property taxes, insurance and electricity, and Dan insisting they could get more—I suggested we compromise, and he finally agreed to $324,900. It really needed to be under $320,000, but that would have to wait.

When establishing a price for a property, sellers—and realtors—need to be aware they are sending a message. Same with counteroffers. What message do you want to send? A list price that is obviously high sends a message that someone is unrealistic or not listening to the facts. (Like $329,900.) Here's the thing about list price: it's a mathematical rule, as is clearly shown in the following pricing pyramid diagram.

71

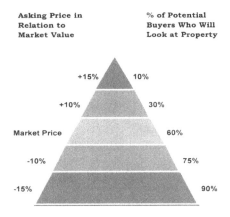

THE REAL ESTATE PRICING
PYRAMID

Asking Price in Relation to Market Value		% of Potential Buyers Who Will Look at Property
+15%		10%
+10%		30%
Market Price		60%
-10%		75%
-15%		90%

The higher you are above market value, the fewer buyers will be interested, and the lower you go, the more buyers are interested. There's a price where every house will sell in a week (or sooner) and that's below market value.

Of course, there are a lot of moving parts. There are three basic types of real estate markets largely based on supply and demand and on statistics:

1. Seller's market—sellers have the advantage because there aren't so many properties on the market.
2. Buyer's market—buyers have the advantage because there are more properties on the market to choose from.
3. Balanced market—neither the buyer nor the seller has the advantage. This is the best kind of market if you are going to sell and buy in the same market condition. It's less stressful.

One factor is the question of how easy it is to sell and how difficult it is to buy. It's all a matter of supply and demand, as in any free market.

Estate Sales...Seriously?

During the economic cycles we all experience, we can find our-selves in a hot seller's market. During 2016 and 2017 in the lower mainland of BC, we had a market like that. You see, each market has its own psychology. During those years we had a shortage of inven-tory, excellent interest rates and many buyers competing for the few available properties. In that hot seller's time, it was easy to sell and for what could look like big bucks, but almost impossible to buy. A seller could get ten (or twenty, or more) competing offers and sell far above asking price, but when they went out to buy, they were now one of the ten, twenty or more competing offers. Prices were going up so fast that pretty soon the big bucks they sold for weren't nearly enough to buy.

Returning to Marcy and Dan's story, if they wanted to sell quickly, I would have told them to list for $309,900 which was a few thousand above market value. At that price, someone would have pounced for sure. But I had Dan on board, and he wasn't ready to go there... yet. He needed time to get the picture. The market condition they were in was a "balanced market slightly in favour of buyers," which is important to know.

Several showings by other agents and many Sunday open houses later, we were still on the market. Feedback from the realtors told us that it was a very lovely place and it showed great, but their buyers didn't want to "low ball." When a place is listed too high, buyers see a market value offer as too low, and many buyers may think there's no point. Also, realtors who know it's listed too high will show it as contrast to a well-priced similar property. In other words, it becomes a high-priced comparable to help sell a realistically priced property.

So it was time for a market update. We met on the phone again, and I emailed any relevant recent activity (area sales since the prop-erty was listed) which all supported my advice. I gave them all the realtor feedback too. After a lot of discussion, we dropped the price to $319,900. Dan said he wouldn't go lower. At least we were in the ballpark now.

More time passed with more showings and more open houses. One sunny Sunday, a realtor brought a lady through. She loved it. It was obvious. It was a nice home. Full kitchen just like in a house and separated bedrooms and bathrooms. As she said, it was great for her and her sister. After the showing, the agent called me.

"Hi Sharon."

"Oh, hi Doug! Thanks for showing my listing today."

"Hey no problem. She's seen a lot of places, and we are wondering if there is any room on the price."

"All I can tell you is bring what you can, and I will work with it. I have two executors to work with, and both are far away. So leave me time to reach them and see what we can agree to."

They sent me an offer: $300,000.

Of course, the job of the buyer is to find out how low the seller will go, and the job of the seller is to see how high the buyer will go. At this point, I always hear the famous words of Sherlock Holmes: "The game is afoot!" In other words, we now have something concrete to deal with—a buyer who wants to buy and an offer in writing. Now is the time to start pulling out the big guns. And the hot button in this case was that the buyer needs a mortgage.

Almost every offer we see is "subject to financing," which means getting a mortgage. A buyer may be prequalified for a certain mortgage amount, meaning their overall financial picture says that they qualify to make the monthly payments on the amount to be borrowed. That mortgage amount plus their down payment (cash on hand) equals the end "purchase price" they can pay. So the buyer has been prequalified and *now the property has to qualify for the requested mortgage amount as well.*

Now let's say we have a seller who wants a higher price than the market indicates. The buyer needs a mortgage to buy it which means the buyer's lender, usually a bank, sends one of those appraisers out to ascertain market value. (Banks and credit unions always have to make sure they are investing their money safely and wisely.) As you know, an appraiser is an independent licensed professional who does a detailed report on the market value of a piece of real estate, and it is often conservative. (In a hot seller's market, when home values are increasing weekly, this can become a real problem.) If the appraiser reports that a buyer is paying too much, the bank will only loan a percentage of the appraised value of the property, meaning that the buyer, if they still want to buy at that price, is going to need a bigger down payment to make up the difference. (And a down payment can't be borrowed. It has to be ready cash or a cash gift from a relative.)

This would be my ammunition for Dan if he was going to dig in his heels. These hard facts could be the key in helping him get realistic. Time, along with lack of results (like no offers), can help someone like Dan accept reality. But sometimes the need to be right and in control is too strong. In this case my difficult seller was referred by a dear friend, so I had to do my best to go the distance and be of service. No matter how stressful this became, I couldn't just walk away from Marcy whom I had come to adore.

I called them with the news.

"Hi Dan and Marcy. Good news, we have an offer. I just emailed it to both of you. Have a look at it, and we will go over it together."

"Wow, that's pretty low."

"Don't worry Dan, that's just their starting place. Not a bad first number."

"We should counter at $315,000."

"We could do that Dan. How is that for you Marcy?"

"What do you think Sharon?"

"Well Marcy, first of all, we don't want to scare them away. I know she loves the place, and she also knows the comparable sale of $305,000. And I can tell you that's what she's expecting to pay. Also, she's getting a mortgage so there will be a bank appraisal, and it will come in at market value which is clearly around $305,000. If she's paying too much above market value, she won't get her mortgage. And that will be the case with any buyer."

Silence.

"So where should we counter?" Dan had accepted an important fact. Whew!

"You want to send a message that says you'd like to find agreement with your buyer, and you want more than $300,000. I suggest $310,000."

So we did. They came back at $303,000. I knew it wasn't enough. We countered back at $308,000. Dan would not take $305,000. It was becoming a "pissing contest" but at least now Dan was in the ballpark with the rest of us. Doug called me.

"Can you give me any advice here?"

"Doug, it's got to be more than the $305,000. See what you can do, and thanks for all your hard work. And patience."

So they came back at $307,000. Now the fun began.

(Dan) "Not good enough. I've thought it over, and I should never have agreed to $308,000."

(Me) "What do you want, Dan?"

"$310,000."

(Marcy) "Dan you're talking about $3,000. That's $1,500 from each of us. We've been on the market for two and a half months, and I want to get this over with. I've done all the work of getting Mom's condo ready and paid for all my travel and hotel. It's a good offer, and we should take it."

"Nope! I'm not selling my mother's house for that price."

(Me) "Ok, shall I call the realtor and tell them no deal?"

(Dan) "I guess you should." He hesitated as though he wanted something. We all hung up. Thirty seconds later the phone rang. It was Marcy.

"Sharon, I`m about ready to kill him. We`re taking that offer. I`ll call you back."

I waited. She did call back.

"Ok Sharon, he agreed. We're taking the offer."

"That's good Marcy. It's a good offer. How did you get him to agree? You are amazing!"

"I paid him off. He was always pretty spoiled. I know how to handle him. I gave him $1,500!"

So, that was what he wanted! Some of her inheritance.

Like I say, it takes all kinds! And Dan was one of them. He got one over on his sister. It was a family issue, and it's the realtor's job to stay out of it. Stay in a neutral position and let them tell you what they want. Sometimes I even have to tell couples who can't agree and who are arguing about what they want to buy, to go figure it out and then let me know. Then I know what to do for them. (One couple never did get back to me. I guess they are still arguing.)

THE LESSON: It's never over 'til it's over. And you never know what it's going to take!

I have seen families torn apart in estate sale situations, including siblings who never speak to each other again. It seems once Mom is gone the claws all come out, and it's every man or woman for him or herself. And the realtor is in the middle of all this, trying to maintain some kind of decorum and to introduce some reality therapy in the face of runaway greed and self-righteousness.

Some of the best advice on this topic came from a career estate lawyer who said, "Don't make your kids your executors." If you must, choose one only. (I was that one for both my mom and dad. My hubby and I do not have our kids as executors.) It could be a trusted friend or a lawyer. They will all, by law, carry out the wishes of the deceased according to the terms of the will. Get legal advice on the laws in your area regarding the roles of the executor and beneficiaries. As my parents' executor, I was so busy handling issues, problems, personalities and legal matters that I was not able to grieve properly as I should have. Make your will very thoughtfully as your last love letter to each other and to your family. Make sure your will and powers of attorney (POAs), including your living will and a healthcare directive or representation agreement, are all in place. You never know when you're going to trip and bump your head and lose capacity.

Let's talk about the matter of legal capacity. For a person to sign a legal document, they must have "capacity" according to the legal definition. An individual does not have legal capacity if they are drunk, certified insane or unable to understand what they are signing. A power of attorney is a legal document where you assign certain rights to someone to represent your interests if you are not able to do so yourself. For example, an elderly person may give power of attorney to a family member or friend to pay their bills for them if they are getting confused. Or perhaps they give someone power of attorney for their health care if they are unconscious or in a coma and cannot represent themselves. This type of power of attorney can be called a healthcare directive or a representation agreement. If you don`t already have a trusted spokesperson and you lose capacity, it's too late. You no longer have legal capacity to sign a legal document. At that point, others may step in, and it may not be your trusted, chosen person. Always have your powers of attorney in place.

THE LESSON: There are many things in life that are better to have and not need rather than need and not have. Your will and powers of attorney are those things. (No good buying insurance after your house has burnt down!)

Meet Tom and Harry

Many years ago, a couple owned a huge and valuable property in a very upscale area. They had two sons. Neither son ever married nor had children. One son lived away in a different province. One stayed in Vancouver at home in the big estate-type property with

Estate Sales...Seriously?

Mom and Dad. When the parents passed away, the estate was divided equally between the two sons. The brother in Vancouver bought a townhouse and lived there for many years until he too passed away. Neither brother ever had a will done. When the Vancouver brother—let's call him Tom—died with no will, his house went to his next of kin in Manitoba, his brother Harry. Eventually Harry died, also without a will. So the search started to locate someone in line to inherit Tom's house.

The government agency that handles such things started looking for a next of kin for Tom and Harry and found some distant cousins. Tom's house should be going to them as next of kin in line, along with anything else owned by Tom and Harry. There were four cousins, all in their eighties and three of them in various stages of dementia and confusion...except for one sharp lady Janine.

Eventually, the Manitoba court declared Janine, who lived in Toronto, to be the legal representative to deal with Tom's house and anything else left behind by both brothers. Then that process had to be repeated in BC where Tom's house was located and which needed eventually to be sold. And all this was moving along at the speed of bureaucracy and the court system. In other words, not quickly! It took a long time and eventually it looked as if Janine would be able to finally sell Tom's house and divide the proceeds, and anything else Tom and Harry had left behind, among the cousins. They were in for a big surprise.

Meanwhile, following the death of Harry, a lady who Harry had been living with for some years claimed to be his common law wife who therefore should be entitled to inherit Tom's house. She started a lawsuit to claim Tom's house for herself. Tom's family had to defend itself, and Janine and her lawyer in Manitoba went to court to do so.

It was a long-drawn-out affair that cost the estate $150,000. In the end, the estate won and for a fascinating reason. The alleged common law wife had refused to produce her tax returns. They were subpoenaed by the court and upon forensic examination were found to reveal her attempted deception: she wasn't his common law wife… she was his landlady! She got caught in her fraudulent attempt to get possession of the house (and any other assets) because she had declared his rent payments in her income for tax purposes with CRA for all those years. One good thing we could say about her? At least she wasn't cheating on her income tax! That lawsuit must have cost her a bundle, and maybe even the court costs as well because she lost the case. Like I keep saying, it takes all kinds!

Eventually, through a referral from a lawyer, I was called on to sell Tom's house. It was full of all his stuff, and it had to be cleared out through lots of donations and trips to the dump done by companies you can hire to do such things. The estate arranged and paid for all that. Fortunately there was money in the estate to pay for it; don't forget that the parents of the two brothers had left them significant wealth in their wills.

I've had a case where the house was sold with everything left in it including furniture, dishes, clothes, art, etc. It was sold "as is, where is," which is a legal term that means the buyer had to accept it full of everything from someone's life. Then the buyer could keep anything they might want and pay to get rid of the rest.

In rare cases where some appliances are not working and there is unknown neglect, we also have to sell the property "as is, where is." We sold Tom's house under that condition, meaning that the buyer is taking it with all its lumps, bumps and things that may be broken or not working; "the seller is making no representations, warrantees or guarantees." The townhouse was in need of paint, repairs, new appliances and some love. Of course that means the property would sell for less than one that was clean, well maintained and ready for occupancy. And it did. It was a good buy for someone who wanted a project for resale or to fix up and enjoy.

So here I was, dealing with a long-distance seller, Janine, who was eighty years old and a delight. Mark Arnstein—a fantastic Toronto realtor—helped me with paperwork, all from his kind and generous heart and with a lot of professionalism. As it turned out, Janine happened to live in his farm area (remember farms?), which I was pleased to hear, and I hope she will call on him when she is ready to sell her house. That was a good connection for him too. (Mark, you are the best! I owe you not one, but many.)

Anyway, we got it on the market, and we did get it sold.

(If you're not sitting down right now, you should be.)

It took nine, yes, NINE years! Nine years from the time Tom died until his house was sold.

During that time, the estate had been paying property taxes, electricity and insurance and even had to pay "empty home tax" on Tom's house. There were huge legal fees, the lawsuit and lawyer fees, and the strata corporation where the townhouse was had a lien against the title for all those years of back strata fees. I asked the lawyer one day if there was enough money left in the estate to cover everything and pay the realtors. She told me, "Yes and it's a good thing the boys' parents left so much money to them in their wills."

THE LESSON: Not taking care of business (responsible "adulting") can end up costing someone an arm and a leg!

As a rule, realtor fees are paid out of the proceeds from the sale. But there are times, like when there are too many mortgages, liens and loans in place, when there may not be enough to pay the realtors when all the financial amounts owing are paid. I have only seen a case like this once in my career. This family wanted to sell and get a bigger place for the parents, kids and newly-moved-in grandparents. They had four mortgages on the house and even what are called chattel mortgages on their possessions (furniture, carpets, dishes, etc.). I don't know if chattel mortgages are even around these days, but that family had NO equity left to pay realtor fees. We showed them how to renovate the little three-bedroom bungalow they had, in order to create the spaces they needed. And I told them not to borrow any more money if they could help it. There was no way I could let them sell. They had no equity at all, so no down payment for the bigger house they had hoped to buy.

Another interesting case is where a couple bought a business from another couple who had made a fortune with that business. The husband stayed on to help the new owner get off to a good start. Over time they both profited greatly from their work together and became close friends. After a time, they went their separate ways but were always close. When the previous owner of the business died, out of gratitude and friendship he left $300,000 to the man who bought his business so many years ago. It was meant to be a lovely surprise. Little did he know that friend had also died and without a will in place. So what happened to the $300,000? It couldn't become part of the late recipient's estate because he didn't leave a last will and testimony. If he had, the $300,000 would have passed through his estate straight to his beneficiaries.

I have been involved over the years with many estate sales, and each one is an exemplary human story. Going forward, you will deal with all kinds of agendas, personalities, emotions, issues and situations. I always see my role as that of the calm in the middle of the storm, trying always to bring everything back to centre and staying on task to find agreement among all the parties involved.

6

What Now? It's All about You

*"A problem cannot be solved
from the same mentality that created it."*
Albert Einstein

All realtors will reach a point where their income can level off.

It's a fact that all human motivation comes from the desire to seek pleasure or avoid pain. And the avoidance of pain wins out every time. That particular trait results in vast amounts of mediocrity in our world. It's called "settling." Once the bills are being paid, the pressure's off. You don't have to do uncomfortable things so much like working overtime and having two or three jobs. You don't have to expand your network and approach people. All that can be uncomfortable for sure. Making sacrifices, like working late nights and weekends or missing event and parties, is not considered "pleasure-seeking activities" for most folks.

Remember our discussion on "comfort zone"? It's a persistent little pest for sure. It can be the result of our upbringing and can involve mistaken beliefs about money and rich people, including beliefs supported by Bible scripture. Like the one about money being the root of all evil. The actual quote is written "The love of money is the root of all evil." There are people all over the world who have benefitted and seen lives changed and saved by funding given by the wealthy. There are legions of stories about wealthy business people, celebrities and corporations whose foundations have funded clean water projects, food, medicine, education, school lunches, free medical and legal services, and scholarship programs. They will tell you that without money (and lots of it), so many good things would never have happened. It takes a lot of hard work to become rich (unless you got your money by inheriting it).

The job is to make friends with money. We can be so conflicted about it; we're afraid of not having it and we are afraid of having it.

Look at people who win a lottery. Studies show that, for a shocking number of them, within a fairly short time (like a year or two) it's all gone, and they are just as broke as they were before…or worse. (I have even heard people say that winning a lottery was the worst thing that ever happened to them. Go figure!) Why is that? Well, for one thing, they are way out of their comfort zone. If the family income was $70,000 a year and all of a sudden they have a million or more all at once (or are being paid out over time as a guaranteed income), they are suddenly on a different planet and don't speak the language. If you ever win a lottery, don't touch the money. Keep doing what you're doing and get lots of advice.

Then, speaking of our relationships with money, there's also our peer group involved—the team you play on, the organization you belong to, your old school buddies or your poker night friends. People have a sort of radar that finds them folks to associate with who are living on the same plane financially, achievement-wise, educationally and lifestyle-wise. We are, after all, herd animals. Social beings. And conforming to the group has been critical to survival in most species. Think about dog and wolf societies. They are highly structured and strictly a hierarchy. You have to know your place and stay in it if you want to survive. To get banished from a herd, flock or pack can mean death. Anyone challenging the alpha creature and the rules of the group can be kicked out and have to go it alone. (It's tough out there!)

Human societies with a class structure are a prime example. These structures are based on history. Take Great Britain, for example. Through most of recorded history there have been the ruling class and the aristocracy who were born into the upper class. They owned all the land and rented it out to the common people who worked their piece of the land and paid taxes to the lord of the manor. They became the working class, and their children were born into the working class, and there they stayed for life. There was no upward mobility in that society. Children had very limited opportunities for education, and even today there are certain schools in any country that are the domain of the upper classes, so to speak. However, with the rise of the middle class, the upper class is no longer determined by right of birth but by other means like family money, and/or scholarly achievement or even excellence in a sport.

The reason I am spending time on this topic is that I want you to take a hard look at your relationship with money. As a realtor, you become an entrepreneur. That means that you get to write your own ticket. You get to decide how much money you want to earn. You can settle, or you can dream bigger. If you had big dreams at one time and life got in the way, start thinking about them again. Being a realtor is an opportunity to revive those hopes and dreams (owning a home you love, driving a car you enjoy, educating your kids, supporting your charity, church or cause, etc.) and not just living to pay the bills. I'm talking planning for retirement with savings, investments and real estate holdings and being able to treat yourself and your family to special times together to make those memories!

The fact is that the majority of realtors, as with most people, get stuck at a certain income level, and it doesn't vary much over time. If you are like me and find this unacceptable, you will learn that it takes many things to avoid a "plateau" in your productivity and income: work, personal growth, vision and new habits.

The need to conform and avoid pain and discomfort can sure enough get in your way. So let's look at a timeframe.

It's commonly held that in the first three years in any business you can pretty much say goodbye to a lot of free time. Don't forget it takes time to get that jet plane off the runway. You need to focus, take training and read books. Make friends with some long hours and steep learning curves. Go easy on yourself when you screw something up. Because you will. And you will learn.

Once you are through the first three years, you will be comfortable with your role. You have something that cannot be replaced or duplicated, and it's called experience. You have developed your database and have come to understand about having a "sphere of influence." This is the beginning of your fan club. These are people who know how good you are at what you do, and they trust you and send you all the referrals they can. They are people with credibility and who are a match for you (maybe your new peer group). And you are starting to make some serious money. You might even have some repeat business by now. That's when a former buyer client needs to sell a couple of years later. And maybe even buy again with you. You have kept in touch and been a pleasant presence in their life, and when they think of moving, they call you! By now you have a business. And if you do, I bet you're paying the bills.

All is moving along. You have accepted the fact that sometimes you work for nothing (you help people look at a few places and they can't afford what they want yet). It's ok, you will make sure they come back to you when they are ready (when they have saved more money or got a raise). You have learned that your activity in January will

86

determine your income in May, June and July, and you have learned that if you're busy, you better get busier. You know for sure that right after you list or sell a property you don't go to the pub to celebrate. You go knock on twenty doors around the property and tell the neighbours. It's called a "tell twenty." (Or at least it was when I got trained. I still call it that.) You have some systems in place, and you are on your way.

Then comes the five-year mark. Anyone who has survived in a business of their own for five years has pretty much made it. Their jet plane is flying well and on course. That includes being a realtor. And here's the best part: the phone now rings for you.

You ought to have a solid client base by now and the knowledge and ability to give people good advice and teach them what they need to know to make good decisions for themselves. You have become their go-to, top-of-mind trusted professional. You have learned what to say and how to say it. In many ways, you have arrived, and you will probably never quit. Real estate can be a life sentence. And a welcome one, at least it is for me. It's truly an honour to become that person in a family's or person's life.

LIFE LESSON: Before you can have much of it, you have to make friends with money. How you find that willingness and worthiness within yourself is an intensely private process. Remember, money is merely a by-product of who you are and what you contribute.

So what does a realtor's life look like at a point like this?

Meet the Harrison Family

Deana, a lovely lady and real estate colleague from long ago, sadly discovered that she had cancer. Although I was a new-ish realtor, she asked me to take over her one and only listing while she was trying to recover from chemo, radiation and alternate healing methods. A long process.

I told her of course I would and that I would split any real estate fees I earned fifty-fifty with her. She protested and I told her that was the only way I would do it so she had to agree. I called Mike and Judy Harrison and made an appointment to meet and look at their home. They gave me a warm welcome, and I adored them from the moment we met. They were recently married and were selling Mike's townhouse with the intention to purchase a detached house. I helped them do both.

During this time, Mike referred his mom, Vera, to me. She was a widow in her late sixties and owned a condo in a concrete high-rise in a busy part of town. Vera wanted a change of scene and not such a big building (thank you very much). She was on an upper floor with a nice view but a long elevator ride and too much time waiting for it to arrive (no matter how many times you pushed the button).

Over the next decade I helped Vera move four times. That was seven "ends" of business. An "end" is realtor lingo for either a listing sold or a buyer who bought. So when I helped Vera sell her high-rise condo that was one end, and when she bought her new place that was one end. During that time, Vera lived in four different apartments, and my hubby Al and I would take Vera out for lunch a couple of times a year. I have some lovely little ornaments in my home that Vera gave me over the years. She was pretty lonely at times, and I tried my best to let her know that I was always available. I would call and check in on her every so often.

Here's the thing about Vera, she probably weighed eighty pounds soaking wet, and she was a Salvation Army Colonel. Her tiny size-zero uniform looked more like doll clothes. I had great respect for her dedication to the unfortunate folks who the Salvation Army minister to. She took these needy and often-inebriated folks into the shelter, fed them, made them say their prayers and put them to bed. (Each year, I can't wait to donate to the Christmas Kettles in her memory.)

Surprise, surprise, we went to her wedding! My little Vera got married at seventy-eight. Her husband, Sib—short for Sibbald—was totally hilarious. They cooked us dinner after they got back from their honeymoon. We laughed until our sides hurt. I always remember Sib telling me while Vera and Al did the dishes, "Sharon, I learned a long time ago that it's important how I talk to girls."

"Oh, I see. Is that how you got Vera to marry you?"

"Absolutely! I told her 'when I look at you, time stand still' instead of 'your face could stop a clock.'" That was Sib! So funny and charming! He lived for about two years of marital bliss, and Vera told me it was the best two years of her life. She went into a care home soon after and passed away within few years. I still have her testimonial on my website.

To whom it may concern,

It is my pleasure to write this letter about my realtor, Sharon Mason. I first met Sharon in 1984 when my son, Michael, recommended her to me. She had acted for him in the sale of his townhouse and in the purchase of a detached house.

I wanted to sell my condo in Richmond and move to a larger apartment in a quieter location. Sharon made it so easy and even fun! Over the years Sharon has helped me to sell and buy a total of 8 times.

As a person who has had no experience with business matters, I have always told Sharon how grateful I am to have an agent who takes the time and has the words to make it all clear to me.

Also, it is a comfort to have someone who gives me advice I can trust. You can be totally confident when you choose Sharon to work with and for you. Bless you, Sharon!

Vera Harrison

Meet Peter Lee

A lovely forty-ish Chinese man called one day. He was calling about a listing I was marketing, and we went to see it. It wasn't right for him, but we had a long chat and we just clicked. You know how that happens; you meet someone and feel like you've known them forever. That was how it was for Peter Lee and me.

He told me that he wanted to buy solid older houses on big lots with hardwood floors, nice doors and windows (French doors a favourite), newer roof and hot water tank and a good furnace. He knew his real estate, and he knew what he wanted.

Peter never gave me his phone number (no email in those days), but he told me I could find him any day of the week at 3 p.m. having coffee and pie at a specific White Spot location. (White Spot is a restaurant chain in BC.)

Peter told me, "When you see a house that has all my choices, you can find me there, and we can go see it."

I helped Peter buy a few houses, and he was always where he said he would be at 3 p.m. every day. Obviously a man of the clock!

One day, a particular property showed up on my radar. It was exactly what Peter Lee loved to buy, and it seemed "lucky."

I learned a lot about helping our brothers and sisters from Hong Kong back in those days before communist China took it over. The late '80s saw a huge influx of Hong Kong citizens pouring into the unique area of Richmond, British Columbia, Canada. This was happening in response to the fact that communist China would be taking over Hong Kong which had been known far and wide as a free market and a free society. Of course, the unknown future was motivating the removal of money—and plenty of it—from the possible reach of a new regime. Canada, always a favourite for immigration, was a popular destination. In addition to the political landscape, Richmond itself offered an ideal feng shui environment. In terms of Chinese values, the symbolism around geographical and domestic patterns and the energy they create couldn't have been better. The Fraser River represented the dragon and Richmond, on Lulu Island, was the eye of the dragon. All ideal for luck, long life, prosperity and everything good!

One thing I learned was about the meaning of numbers. One that I live by to this day is the favoured number eight. Two eights were good and three were even better. Today, as I write this book, my address has four eights in it, and I couldn't be happier. Some of my favourite listing prices have a couple of eights in them, like $568,800 or $1,288,000. I love those happy little eights.

The property I wanted to show Peter Lee was everything he wanted, and it happened to be my listing. It was listed for $288,800. (Of course it was!) I showed up at the White Spot, and there he was as per usual. Coffee and apple pie were on order. He folded the paper he was reading and invited me to sit down and join him in pie and coffee. I was delighted to do so.

After we ate, we drove to the house in question which was nearby. He loved it, and we went to my office, also nearby, to write up an offer.

I told Peter I would be presenting the offer to my sellers in a couple of hours at their home and would get back to him. He had some errands to run and said he would come to the house and wait in his car. It was a full-price offer that was happily accepted by my sellers. I went out to Peter in his car to give him the copy of the accepted offer. I had to talk about the eights, I couldn't help it.

"Here you go Peter. Congratulations, it's a good house. And I think it's your lucky day."

"Oh, what do you mean?"

"Well it is August 8, 1988, or 08/08/88. Doesn't get much better than that!"

He looked at me with a little grin and said, "Sharon, I think it's your lucky day too." We both had a hearty laugh, and that's when I fell in love with eights.

as the last time I saw Peter. I don't know where he went, but he was never at the White Spot at 3 p.m. again. I popped back in there from time to time, but he was never to be seen. I even asked the waiters if he had been in but they said he had not. They all remembered him too, as a wonderful gentleman. Wherever you are Peter, I think of you often.

If you have these kinds of relationships with people, you can become a real estate rock star. You can make a life and a living serving your clients and the people you meet as you go through life. And you can break out of your comfort zone into a new level of significance and also of income. You can rest on your plateau (and there's nothing wrong with that) or you can take ownership of your right to fly, your right to make a difference, and bring your desire to serve, your A-game and your integrity to shine as only you can by being more of you and not holding back.

I refer over and over again to Marianne Williamson's wonderful incantation (that's what I call it, an incantation because it can make you cry) from her brilliant bestseller *A Return to Love* because it can touch your soul and give you permission to shine as you are meant to. The poem "Our Deepest Fear" has been an inspiration to many. Here is an excerpt:

> *"Our deepest fear is not that we are inadequate.*
> *Our deepest fear is that we are powerful beyond measure.*
> *It is our light, not our darkness, that most frightens us."*

I encourage you to find this moving incantation and keep it handy as a reminder to pay attention to that voice within that is calling you to your greatness.

Meet the Dog Who Cried

A delightful, young couple Phil and Marion asked me to come over and talk to them about selling. They had seen my ads and signs around the neighbourhood. They had a nice three-bedroom town-house in our small town of Ladner, BC. We met and they showed me around. I was very familiar with the property so we sat down to talk price and selling strategy. Then I heard the familiar sound of doggy claws on a door. My new clients excused themselves and arrived back in the room with a gorgeous golden retriever named Ernie. Ernie sat down next to me and listened to our conversation for a few minutes and then rested his chin on my knee.

"We've never seen him do that before. Is he bothering you?"

"No, not at all. I love dogs! They are some of my favourite people."

After a bit, Ernie disappeared into the kitchen and returned with a pull toy. Now he rested that on my knee and looked up at me with the big, brown hopeful eyes of an eternal optimist. Marion interrupted our chat.

"Excuse me Sharon, Ernie only brings that toy to us and Phil's dad. He really loves you."

I can't tell you how flattered I feel when an animal likes me. (Or a baby.)

"I really like you too, Ernie!" and I pulled on the toy. Dogs love that game. He had a tail that could clear off a coffee table in one swipe.

I listed their house, and every time I went there, Ernie got his special toy. Of course I fell in love with Ernie, and it was mutual. A few weeks later I came down with a ferocious flu bug and was flat out in bed with a fever. I called Phil and Marion and left a message on their answering machine telling them that if we had any showings, I wouldn't be there for a few days, and if we needed a realtor present, one of my colleagues would be in attendance.

When Marion got home from work a couple hours later, she called me.

"Sharon, I hope you're feeling better and that I'm not calling at a bad time, but I had to tell you what just happened. I started playing your message, and as soon as Ernie heard your voice he went and got that toy and he sat in front of the answering machine whimpering. He could hear you, but you weren't there. He kind of flopped down on the floor and looked at the machine crying."

"Oh my goodness Marion, I don't know what it is between Ernie and me but maybe it's from another life."

"I have no idea, but he's crazy about you. And by the way, he was a big reason we decided to list with you. He's a great judge of people!"

I was touched beyond words. After their home sold, they moved to another part of the country, and Ernie was gone out of my life. We shared lots of doggy hugs and kisses, and he and his mommy and daddy are forever in my heart.

Meet Hilda and Shandy

A very special client of mine was a sweet English lady named Hilda Scurr. I listed her charming home for sale, and we became good friends. I first visited Hilda just before Christmas. The decorations were beautifully traditional, and the whole house radiated a warm and cozy feeling which I felt the minute I walked in. As in any respectable English home, we sat down to tea and scones. Tea was served in proper china teacups and poured from an elegant pot through a strainer. Loose tea, of course. No bags for Hilda! She was a real lady.

The other "lady" in the house was a stunningly gorgeous collie named Shandy. She looked just like Lassie. Hilda must have brushed that dog's shiny coat at least once a day. Shandy snoozed on the floor during tea time. Then she followed us around to help show me the property. It was immaculate and so welcoming I almost didn't want to leave when the time came.

We returned to the den to discuss the topic of selling. Being so close to Christmas and understanding about family plans, I recommended we wait and come on the market in January. She liked that idea. The house was too big for her now, and it was time to downsize. When we were done with business talk, it was time for the unexpected entertainment.

Until now, Shandy had been a happy, smiley presence. Little did I know what was coming! Hilda had this adorable English accent which I cannot share adequately in print so use your imagination. "Shandy, show Sharon your purse." Shandy trotted out of the room and returned with her purse. The semi-circular handle would normally go over one's forearm, but in this case it was centred in her mouth. She gave it to me, smiled (I don't know what else to call it) and wagged expectantly. She look at me and then the purse a couple of times. I realized that I would have to open it because it had a gold clasp on the top and she had no thumbs. So I did. She looked in the purse and wagged harder.

"Well Shandy! You have quite the purse here! Let's see what you've got."

(An excited yelp.)

"Oh my…car and house keys, lipstick, a change purse and a cotton handkerchief." Of course no English lady would be without one. And this had an S embroidered on it. I made the appropriate oohs and aahs, and Shandy was delighted that I understood her status in the household. Then Hilda spoke.

"Shandy put your purse away and show Sharon your Christmas present." (Please try to imagine how she rolled her letter 'r' oh so slightly…adorable!)

Shandy took the purse handle gently in her mouth, vanished into the living room where the beautifully decorated tree stood, and returned with a gift-wrapped box, carrying it by the bow on top. Once again I expressed great enthusiasm for the fact that it looked lovely and even rattled a bit.

"My goodness Shandy, I bet you just can't wait 'til Christmas morning!"

(Another quick yelp.) OMG, we seemed to be having a conversation!

"Put your present back under the tree now Shandy." And she did.

I helped Hilda move three times over the years, and we became close friends. She was a shining example to me of someone who had gone through a lot of painful losses in her life and somehow carried on with a lovely heart and an appreciation of life. When Shandy died it was a terrible loss, but she got on with living life to the fullest. That was Hilda.

Meet Lorraine McCloy

Near the beginning of my real estate career, I met this wonderful woman Lorraine. She had three amazing young daughters: Karen, Cheryl and the Baby Lynda who was a tiny toddler about two years old. They owned a charming three-bedroom split level and needed a fourth bedroom. Lorraine kindly asked me to help in the process, and I was delighted to do so. We put their current home on the market and started to look for the new one. We had fun. While the two older girls were in school, Lorraine and I would take Lynda and look at properties that were for sale. Lorraine was one of the most intuitive buyer clients I have ever known. She would walk into a house, and within thirty seconds she pretty well knew if it was speaking to her or not. I related to her process because I'm like that myself with my own house hunting.

I had a buyer once, Lilly, who was also intuitive. We actually walked into a house one day and, still standing in the front foyer, she said, "This is the one Sharon. I'm buying it."

"Don't you want to make sure it has indoor plumbing first?" We laughed. She bought the house. No kidding that it takes all kinds!

Back to Lorraine, we got an offer on the nice split level, and soon we had completion and possession dates. Time to get serious. We had seen enough houses to know the right one when it showed up on the market. Sure enough, as often happens, the right house showed up right when we needed it. This one was an exceptional home with four huge bedrooms; an attractive Tudor on a cul-de-sac and very close to schools. Perfect. A super nice property. We gathered up Lynda, the tiny two-year-old, and headed right over.

When I made the appointment the listing agent told me there would be a cat in the laundry room that usually just sleeps all the time and please don't let him out. No problem. I love cats. So away we went.

The minute we entered the house, it just felt right to both of us. We strolled through to the kitchen and family room and headed for the laundry room. Indeed, as promised, there was the cat. A handsome orange fellow asleep on top of the dryer on a stack of fluffy towels. He jumped down off the dryer and, oh my goodness, he was huge! He looked more the size of a bobcat or a small puma.

We swear to this day that he was twice the size of Lynda. In fact, we learned later that he weighed in at forty-three pounds. Yes indeed, about twice the size of Lynda! Fortunately, he was merely heading for the couch where he flopped over onto a soft cushion and started to purr, not really interested in us at all, thank goodness. We could see that he had no idea of his place at the top of most food chains. We were also happy to see an empty cat food dish that read "Goliath" or "Attila" or some such cautionary epithet. The fact that it was empty, we speculated, meant that he had been fed and tiny Lynda was out of danger!

That was in 1984. And in November of 2020, I helped them sell that house after thirty-six years of making memories in it. Somehow Lorraine and I had lost touch over the years. In 2018, one of those real estate miracles happened. I had a townhouse listed in a charming age-restricted complex. (Age-restricted means that there is an age limit to live there. For example, 45+ or 55+ are common. Kids can visit but not live there permanently.) I had done an open house there and, of course, lots of neighbours came by to check it out. Little did I know that one of the neighbours was a long-time friend of Lorraine. A few days later, Lorraine was at her house for coffee.

"Lorraine, whenever you sell the house, you should buy here. We would be neighbours. Wait a minute, the realtor had an open house, and I've got the paper." She produced the open house flyer for my listing.

"Oh my God, it's Sharon!"

"What? Who's Sharon?"

Pointing at my photo, "It's Sharon. She's my realtor! I need her!"

I am forever grateful to that dear lady for keeping my flyer. The next morning my phone rang, and when I saw McCloy on the call display my heart skipped a beat and the goosebumps happened. I could not have been happier if I had won the lottery! Since then, Lorraine and I have been as close friends as ever and have had lots more laughs.

We got that lovely Tudor house sold and found a dream condo to purchase. The whole family pitched in to sort through thirty-six years of life and memories. (Downsizing is quite a journey!) I can't tell you how honoured I have been to be of service to these dear people.

These kinds of stories are part of what has kept me in real estate over the years. It's the richness of the humanity—all these amazing people and their stories—that has taught me so much and has allowed me to appreciate the journey and my ability to help with such an important aspect of life: their home. There is some opinion out there that it's "just business." Not so for me. How can it be just business? I am in their home, knowing their family, knowing about their hopes and dreams, their struggles and often their secrets. And I am helping them find a home. It's intensely personal. For me, it is business plus a huge amount of heart. It's my intention to treat their transaction as if it were my own. And it's not about money. It can't be. As my clients' agent, it is my pledge to have no agenda of my own; my agenda has to be their agenda. If I think their agenda is not wise or is ill-advised for them right now, I advise them not to go forward.

In fact, I am always telling people I meet who already have a property that they should try to keep it; to see if they can make the move they want and still keep that asset (for example, rent it out and let your tenants pay off the mortgage, or accumulate assets). Don't get rid of the house if you don't have to. Folks are so surprised when I tell them that.

They say, "Aren't you a realtor? Aren't you supposed to want to sell our house?"

I say, "If you want someone to treat you like that, it won't be me." And we laugh.

The secret is to put your head down and go to work serving people. Do the right thing at all times. My dear husband of more than forty years has asked me, "Do you have any idea how much money you made last month?"

"I have no idea, and I don't want to know." It cannot be the issue. Money and winning production awards cannot be the main thing, especially if you want to sleep nights. The secret is to know what you stand for and draw your line clearly in the sand.

THE LESSON: As long as you're a realtor, you will enjoy a wonderful parade of humanity coming into your life. It becomes a lifestyle and an opportunity to grow and expand, and to serve. And it gives you amazing stories to tell and even put in a book!

7

The Plateau...
Resting on Your Laurels or Not

*"[...] the sooner you make the transition
to becoming intentional about your personal growth,
the better it will be for you, because growth compounds and
accelerates as you remain intentional about it."*
John Maxwell

Remember my "tears in my ears" moment when I was lying on my back crying my eyes out over my farm? I think they call that a dark night of the soul. Mine was on a hot afternoon but it's the same thing. A crossroads! Decision time. Sink-or-swim time. A time to quit? Keep going? Put a time limit on it? Obviously, I decided to keep going for at least another six months.

There's a philosophy called "one more door" and it is a powerful idea. The day I knocked on Mary Elias's door when I was about to call it a day, was my one more door. Here's a fact: So often massive success has come just after someone has faced up to the temptation to quit. There are a lot of old sayings and chestnuts about those ideas.

"It's always darkest before the dawn."

"If at first you don't succeed, try, try again."

Yeah, yeah, yeah, we've heard it all before! But here's something you may not be aware of…the concept of "failing forward." Look for John Maxwell's book by that name. He has written a whole library of brilliant books and New York Times bestsellers that teach about success and leadership. He teaches us the welcome knowledge that everyone who has achieved anything significant has experienced "failure." They could have quit and justified it to themselves, but they didn't. For example, there's the famous story of Thomas Edison. While trying to invent the electric light bulb, he had 1,100 failed experiments. His attitude was that he had discovered 1,100 ways that didn't work. The next time you turn on a light, be grateful that Tom failed forward!

About three months ago I was having lunch with a "long-time" friend (we decided to remove "old friend" from our vocabulary) and here's how it went:

"Sharon, you are always so positive. What do you do about your failures?"

"I don't see those as failures."

"What do you see them as?"

"I see them as lessons. I look at how it happened, how I contributed to it and what I could have done differently. I see these situations as opportunities to become more aware and become better."

"Yes, I see, that is a better way. I'm going to quote you."

Turn a negative into a positive. The dichotomy says that you either win or lose. I go with the concept that you win or *learn*. And incidentally, winning can also come with big lessons attached to it.

So much of personal growth is being a good student of your own life. Our lives are full of decisions, and each decision is attached to a consequence. Where we find ourselves at any given moment in life is the result of all the decisions we have made along the way. Some decisions may have seemed insignificant at the time, but nonetheless they have contributed to the present moment. Our paths are made up of a series of those connected dots.

Once we see it this way, we are more able to take ownership of wherever we find ourselves. Many folks wander through life with no objective other than the very immediate ones like making it to Friday, getting to watch the game on Sunday and not getting fired. (Or maybe getting fired and going on EI.) Some professionals call this lifestyle "drifting." These souls drift from one thing to another, and sometimes it works out, but unfortunately it can backfire. The story of each life is a tale of small decisions and choices made repeatedly day upon day, year upon year.

The opposite is a life of "intention"—a life of setting targets, objectives and goals. (Maybe graduating from high school, getting a diploma or a degree or starting a career. Buying a house, saving money for a purpose or for future retirement. Getting married or moving in together. Planning a trip around the world. Starting a family. Starting a business. Planning for the future.) And then taking steps towards the fulfillment of those intentions.

Then there are the folks who live with one foot in each zone. I am not judging anyone here; just pointing out that there are choices and their consequences.

Which path is chosen is a function of many things including the person's background, childhood home influences, expectations from parents, teachers and coaches, and sibling rivalry. (Also known as your peer group. Did you know that if you look at the incomes of the five people you are around the most, your income will tend to reflect the average of those incomes? It's that comfort zone thing again!)

We all know dear people who have chosen one of these lifestyle choices: "drifting" or "intentional" or some combination.

When you are a realtor, you are likely moving toward, or are already in, the intentional category. Your longevity in the business will depend upon it. And that takes three main things:

1. Knowing your business including the market, the laws and rules of conduct, and the way to do research and paperwork such as listing documents, offers, and counteroffers.
2. People skills including strong communication skills (listening and speaking but mostly listening), teaching skills, understanding body language, managing expectations, negotiating, handling questions and concerns, and being an advisor.
3. Yourself.

The first two? Lots to learn and doable.

Number three? Another story altogether. This is where personal development and self-management show up, as well as the ability to handle adversity (possessing resilience) and to detach from outcomes (the big one for many of us).

These are huge topics and must be addressed. Personal development—such as emotional intelligence, self-control, self-discipline, persistence, focus, vision, faith and more—is vital in our lives and in any pursuit of success. Libraries are filled with thousands of books on these and other formidable topics for helping human beings fulfill their potential for excellence, balance and well-being. There are many teachers, coaches, gurus and spiritual leaders you can study with.

Always remember this great quote by John Dryden and take it to heart: *"We first make our habits, then our habits make us."* He was a seventeenth-century English poet and literary leader of his day. Just goes to show that a great truth is a great truth. In fact, I believe this is more true today than it was back in the 1600s. Back then the big habit was snuff—a tobacco product that could be inhaled through the nose or chewed. Seems pretty innocent by today's standards!

I encourage you (and everyone) to be intentional in your life about all those little decisions that count. Like the song lyrics from Depeche Mode that point out "Everything counts in large amounts. So come on, I'm talkin' to you!"

There are two types of habits:
1.   Exterior habits—our behavior
2.   Interior habits—our thoughts and self-talk

Which of the two do you think are the most powerful and influential habits? If you said number two, you are right! That inner chatter will win out every time. There is always a negative voice, the inner critic, and there is also the positive voice. The negative voice almost always rules the roost, and the battle we all are engaged in is to turn down its volume. You can't shut it up altogether and, at the same time, turn up the volume on the positive side, which doesn't get much notice as a rule. It's a muscle that needs exercise. People, therefore, are at war with themselves. So, here's the question...who is winning?

In most people's lives it's the negative voice. Old cartoons are full of images of a devil on one shoulder tempting the poor victim to be naughty, irresponsible or nasty, and on the other shoulder there's a sweet, little angel offering encouragement and appealing to the good nature and conscience of the character in question. Should I binge watch Netflix all night or study for my exam and/or finish that report for work? Truth be told, it's always more entertaining and interesting when the "victim" chooses the one the devil is suggesting. We all have it going on and many times a day.

Dr. Deepak Chopra tells us the scientific fact that every thought we think, everything we tell ourselves and everything we say affects every cell in our bodies. Chemicals are released and neurological pathways are established. Did you know that tears of joy and tears of sorrow are completely different from each other chemically?

Always remember, thoughts are things. Whether you think you can or you think you can't…you're right.

What about your own "self-talk"? It's very important to start identifying that little devil and to start feeding your mind the good stuff. Don't let those messages take you out because they can. And it's a constant vigil until you become aware of the damage you are allowing. Quite often those voices aren't just in our heads. I actually hear people say them out loud: I'm so stupid! I never get anything right! What's the matter with me? I forget/lose everything. I'm such a slob!

And look out if they receive a compliment!

"Wow, you look great!"

"Had your eyes checked lately?"

Hmmm…I won't be trying that again. (Ouch!) I find it such a graceful thing when someone accepts a compliment with "Thank you" or "Thank you, you're very kind."

Yes, it's all about personal development and working towards more of all the good things. There's a fascinating book called *Feed the Good Dog* by Paul McCabe. This will really help with that inner war we all face. Learn about the power of affirmations (when used correctly) and the joys of a vision board that keeps your goals and intentions in front of you. Get a cork board and some push pins and arrange photos of whatever your dreams and goals are. Check in on it regularly, the more often the better.

In the early 1980s, before I got into real estate, the biggest annual income I had ever received was $15,000 as a schoolteacher. Things were a fraction of what they cost today, so you can imagine that my idea of earning $20,000 was quite a significant jump—25%! Find your vision and stay focused.

Thinking back to the five people you hang around with the most (it's important to understand the power of your peer group; it's called your comfort zone), let's say a person is comfy earning $50,000 a year. If they start earning $5,000 to $10,000 less or more than that, it gets uncomfortable. The "herd" they travel with all make around the same, and there can be a pecking order based on income levels within the "herd" or peer group. If an individual starts to be different and shows up in a new way, the peer group may not like it. (Sometimes it's even your family.) And it's not always to do with money either. You could just be starting something new and unfamiliar and "not like you." They may rain on your parade, and that can be hard to take. In fact, it often stops people before they get started.

At this time, I must take a moment to tell you about the crab pot. Yes, crab pot. Ever been crabbing? They sink crab traps with bait into the ocean and leave them for a day or so. The crabs, of course, go after the bait and are caught. They are generally put in a big tub, several crabs all in there together. There's always one who tries to get out by clambering up the sides and reaching for the top. (Now that's gotta be one determined crab with a strong sense of self-preservation!) But guess what? The other crabs come over and pull him back down into the tub! (And this is a fact.) People can be the same in trying to keep the herd together. Beware of the crab pot.

I think we all know stories of famous and successful people who have folks around them asking when they are getting a "real job." Anyone who has been on the planet for a while will have had a chance to observe this tendency. So, what will you do about your naysayers? (If you don't have any naysayers around you, you are privileged indeed.) Make sure you're around those who encourage you and support your dreams, goals and intentions.

Now for me, when I started to recognize my new peer group— my realtor colleagues making six figures or on their way to it—I didn't realize the impact it would have on me. I would have to expand my comfort zone and I didn't realize it.

Some people call it "shedding your old skin." And you will over time. If you are already a realtor, you will have seen yourself change. Things you used to worry about and stress over are no longer such a big deal, and your belief in yourself and your confidence has grown. This happens to everyone in various ways and in various time frames, but it will happen.

So as we go forward into your next three or four years, know that personal development is everything! Read, take seminars or weekend intensives, and get coaching and mentoring. Be a sponge and soak up everything you can for your whole career. Be more disciplined in your habits, especially the inner ones. Be 1% better every day at looking after yourself and your clients. And always bring kindness and love, especially to yourself!

LIFE LESSONS: Always find the lessons in the good and the not so good. Stay committed to your purpose and be careful who you're hanging around with and who you're listening to. Keep your focus looking forward and protect your energy.

8

Don't Push Your Luck! You Talkin' to Me?

"Sometimes they just need a pie in the face."
Stuart Wilde

Life is always trying to teach us lessons. If we try to ignore the lessons or refuse to learn them, life may find more intrusive ways of trying to teach us. Choosing a life as a realtor is sure to throw more life lessons at you and often in a more intense fashion.

One of my lessons had been around standing up for myself, for my rights and my dignity, and not letting people treat me unfairly or inappropriately. After being in my new peer group of realtors—a group of self-reliant entrepreneurial individuals—I began to develop a sense of my own power and my own self-reliance. After a few years of success, I had learned how to draw a line in the sand. The message I emanated became *I am a total sweetheart until you cross me or try to put one over on me and my clients. If you try it, you better look out! If you choose to play dangerous like that, you will be sorry. I have claws.* I assure you, you don't often need those claws. But here's the fact: when you have claws and when you know how to use them, you hardly ever have to. You have that stance in life that says *don't even try it!*

Meet Brad, Mary and Brian

I had listed a home for sale, and my clients, Brad and Mary, were a dear couple who had been married forever and had that kind, homey atmosphere around them at all times. They needed to get away from their stairs. Brad did have a stair lift to help him up and down, but it was time for one-level living. They had found a perfect spot near some family members in a small town further east in the Fraser Valley of British Columbia. We were selling their home in Richmond, BC, just outside of Vancouver.

One evening, Brian, a successful young realtor from a large and well-known company in the area, called to tell me he had written an offer on Brad and Mary's home. His company had been trying to recruit me to leave Realty World and join up with their company. In fact, as I eventually learned, they had assigned a veteran lady realtor to recruit me over to their side of the fence. I didn't like their side of the fence, so I was totally resistant to being recruited by them, or any other office for that matter. They weren't the only one. I was totally happy right where I was. I loved the Realty World philosophy of humility and down-to-earth service.

Brian and I set up a time to meet at the house to present the offer to my clients. When I arrived, Brian was already sitting at the kitchen table with my sellers. We had agreed to meet outside, but he was early and had rung the bell, deciding to jump the gun. Hmmm… Not really protocol but I decided to let that go for now.

The offer he had written was face down on the kitchen table; a traditional place for it to be. I sat down opposite Brian, and my sellers were at each end of the table. Brian, unfortunately, spoke.

"So Sharon, have you decided to come work with us [his company]? You're probably almost good enough."

Whaaat? Almost good enough? Wait a minute! Totally over my line in the sand. And totally unacceptable. My loyal and dedicated clients and I exchanged glances.

"Brian, you are excused. Go outside and wait in your car, and we will let you know if we want to hear anything from you. Give that offer to me, and I will let you know what my clients wish to do with it."

My eyes were burrowing through his skull. He got the vibe and left. We heard the front door close behind him. Brad and Mary burst into a brief round of applause.

Brad spoke. "Sharon, that was awesome! He is obviously some kind of jerk."

Mary said, "You sure put him in his place!"

"Thanks, he needed to be put in his place, and I'm not through with him yet."

We countered the offer, raising it $5,000. It was actually a pretty good offer. Ours was a fair counteroffer. I thanked my clients and said I would get back to them that evening and that I thought their counteroffer would fly.

When I got outside Brian was standing under a streetlamp. I didn't give him a chance to speak.

"Take this counteroffer and get it accepted, and fax it (oh the 1990s) to me tonight. And by the way, if you ever, and I mean ever, speak to me like that again, especially in front of my clients, I guarantee that you will have a new profession. You will be singing with the Vienna Boys' Choir, and I guarantee that you will be singing soprano."

I got in my car and left him standing there looking sheepish. An hour later, by fax, I had the accepted counteroffer in my hand, and I also had a call from guess who. Right, Brian.

"Sharon, I'm really sorry. I shouldn't have said that. If you would come to my house in the morning, I want to cook breakfast for you and apologize properly."

"Ok Brian, I accept your apology. I will see you in the morning."

"Ten o'clock?"

"Sure."

I went there in the morning, and we had waffles and really good coffee. We were ok with each other, and it was over. It takes a real adult to apologize and mean it. I respected his maturity and sincerity, and I think he learned a lesson about arrogance and unprofessional behavior. We remained friends and good colleagues for many years. He wasn't one of those guys who can't stand a successful woman. I have run into that unfortunate situation but blessedly not often.

It can really surprise people when you respond with a strong, assertive truth. They usually fold like a house of cards. And they should!

THE LESSON: Truly, people treat us the way we teach them to or let them. Here's the thing, once we are clear on our boundaries, we have an aura that says *don't even try it!* Don't worry, it can take time to activate your how-dare-you button, but it will happen.

Meet David

David owned a rental house. His tenants had been there for years. He wanted to sell it, and he asked me to help as I had been selling a lot of homes around the area. We met and I took a look at the house. He had a tenant who was pretty grouchy, and I could see the handwriting on the wall. The tenant wasn't going to cooperate; he didn't want to move. Hmmm… That means the place is going to look a mess, likely not be clean, maybe smelly, maybe even have a cranky dog or there may rarely be a time we can arrange to show the house. Tenants sometimes do what they can to sabotage a sale…like not being home when the realtor arrives with potential buyers.

I talked to David about these issues and asked him to make a deal with the tenant, like offer to pay for his move or something to motivate some positive cooperation. He didn't take my advice, but I tried hard to sell that house for six long months anyway. Also the price was a little too high and, as you now know, price is a major factor. We let the listing expire, and the tenant got his way (not moving).

A word about how a listing expires: When a property goes on the market, there is a listing contract between the seller and the real estate brokerage. It has a start date and an expiry date. On the stated expiry date, the contract terminates at 11:59 p.m. That date may be extended in writing, but in this case it was best to let it expire.

I always kept in touch with David. I felt he would eventually sell that house, and I planned to still be his realtor. (Long-term thinking!) A couple of years later he called me. The tenant was finally moving! Ok, a perfect time to sell! The tenant would be gone in a couple of weeks, so we could have access to the house, and it would be clean and free of the tenant's messy stuff. Once the house was empty, we had it cleaned, and I had the photos taken. The paperwork was done, and we were ready to go. Of course, David now had no rental income to help with expenses like a mortgage payment, insurance, heat and electricity and property taxes. This time he was more motivated to price it smartly. And we did.

Very predictably, it sold in a couple of weeks. We got a full-price offer, and the deal was done. That was on a Sunday night.

Every Monday morning we had our office meeting, and this was the Monday after David's house was sold. At our weekly meeting, we always heard about new office listings and "needs and wants" (what our colleagues were looking for on behalf of their buyers). We also had some training and team building. Then we all piled into cars and went on tour. We all had a list of the newly listed properties we were going to see. It just so happened that there were four brand-spanking-new realtors going on tour for the first time. As a senior team member and a good coach for new realtors, I was asked by my manager if I would take the newbies on tour and give them a bit of training and advice. I loaded them all into my big Lincoln Town Car and away we went.

I had a car phone. It had the hands-free feature of course and a speaker in the car. When I received a call, the conversation was broadcast for all to hear.

(Ring…ring…)

"Hello. Sharon speaking."

"Hi Sharon, it's David."

"Oh, hi David! I am so happy that you got such a good offer last night and that we got your house sold!"

"Well, that's what I want to talk about."

"Ok, what's up?"

"Well, I was thinking that since the house sold so fast, just a couple of weeks, that I shouldn't have to pay the whole realtor fee."

Uh oh, he wanted to give me a pay cut! Hmmm…

"Just a minute now, let me see if I've got this right. You think that because I got your house sold quickly so that you wouldn't have to continue paying your mortgage, insurance, taxes, heat and electricity with no rental income, I should agree to less pay? Have I got that right?"

"Well, yeah."

"David, David, David [said very slowly], I'm really disappointed in you."

"Why?"

"I really thought you were a better person than that."

Silence.

"Have you forgotten all the work and effort I put in trying to sell that house two years ago? I had to deal with your difficult tenant and spent many hours and many dollars doing my best for you for six months."

I could literally feel the tension building in the car. Those new realtors were all holding their breath and maybe even starting to sweat.

"I'm very disappointed that you feel that way. Actually, I probably deserve a bonus."

More silence.

"Well, I thought I'd ask."

"You asked. Anyway, I have to go. I'm in the middle of taking a car full of new realtors to look at listings this morning."

During this entire conversation, I had been driving in traffic. That's how cool and confident I had finally learned to be. I have to confess, I felt very powerful. I was so clear on the boundary he had crossed. No way, David. He was off my Christmas list.

When I hung up the phone, the stress level in the car was palpable. Someone spoke.

"Oh geez Sharon. I could never say that kind of stuff to anyone." They all agreed.

I said, "Oh yeah? Just wait." And I meant it.

I can't remember if I scared any of them away that day, but they just had a small taste of what personal empowerment can look like. They didn't know that I had been raised to be a super people-pleaser; "the disease to please." So many folks I know have it. One of the main symptoms is weak boundaries, or none at all, and a total absence of assertive behavior. It's a hard way to live and reflects a big need to be liked; to be seen as a good person, a nice person. It can be a long, hard journey to get free of what others think of us. Eventually I came to see that what matters is what I think of myself. If I had gone along with David's wishes and not been paid fairly, as agreed, for all my efforts, professionalism and dedication, I would have sold out and let myself down badly. And I would have set a bad example for the new realtors. Realtors earn every penny and more. It was right for me to take care of me. I had taken care of him enough, and it wasn't even appreciated. (And, confession time, I have to admit I did enjoy making him squirm.)

LIFE LESSON: Know what your boundaries are. Make sure they are fair but firm. Don't compromise; every time you do, a little piece of you withers and you lose personal power.

Meet Julie and Ed

Julie and Ed bought a house in the late 1980s. Ed painted the interior of the house and put in new laminate floors throughout the main part of the house. It was a basement-entry two-level, and it was sparkling clean. In 1989, at the height of the migration from Hong Kong into Richmond, buyers were flocking into my area to buy houses and bringing lots of cash. We knew a plane load of buyers was flying in that week to purchase real estate. That was the week I put Julie and Ed's place on the market. The timing couldn't have been better. They had recently paid $170,000. The house needed work, and Ed had done it, and now, in this hot seller's market, we could list it for $259,000. They were thrilled! That's how good the market was; one of those hot seller's markets.

One more thing I failed to mention, Julie and Ed had already bought a new place. They bought a home to move to before they sold their current home. Sometimes that is ok to do, but often it is not a good idea. It's a question often asked: Should you sell first or buy first? A good and important question, but more on that topic later.

Soon a realtor brought a buyer from one of the folks who had arrived from Hong Kong. The house looked so good they offered $250,000. All cash; no need to get a mortgage approved, which is always awesome. It was a realtor colleague from my office who brought the offer to us. We all sat at the kitchen table (where most family decisions are made). The offer was strong. However, the buyer wanted the fridge, stove, washer and dryer. We all took a look at the appliances. They were very old but still working fine. We all agreed that if you wanted to sell them as used appliances you might get about $1,200. Hmmm.

Julie dug in her heels and said, "No, he's not getting my appliances." I couldn't believe my ears. We sat there for hours trying to make it clear that it wasn't worth losing this deal for $1,200 worth of used appliances. No way; she was adamant. Ed wanted to take the offer. It was getting ugly. The buyer's agent told them that her buyer wouldn't go any higher. He wanted the house, but that was as high as he would go.

This hot seller's market couldn't last forever, and the number of houses for sale in the area had been increasing steadily. Once word got out that you could sell for big bucks in our area and move further out of town and buy much cheaper, well, of course a lot of folks wanted to get on that gravy train. We pointed all that out to Julie, but no way was she budging. So they let the offer go. And, don't forget, they had already bought. They would need the money from this house to complete their purchase coming up in about ninety days.

"Ok Julie and Ed, as your agent I am officially telling you that if you can't sell for this much in the future, do not blame me."

"No Sharon, we won't. If we can't sell it, we'll just rent it out."

"Ok then. You're planning to hang on and rent it out so there's no point in me calling you for a market update if the market changes. We will just leave it as it is, and if you can't sell for enough, you will rent it out to a tenant. Have I got that right?"

"Yes, that's right."

During the next month, what I had predicted and explained to Julie and Ed actually happened: the market changed. A ton of new listings came on the market, and it quickly became a buyer's market. Lots of properties were listed now, so buyers had a lot to choose from and bargain for. In accordance with our agreement, I left Julie and Ed alone. Then all hell broke loose.

(Ring…ring…)

"Hello, Sharon speaking."

It was Julie, and she was definitely in the red zone. "Hello. Why haven't you called us? No one is looking at our house. We need to sell. You're supposed to be our realtor!" She was fuming.

"Julie, are you at home?"

"Yes."

"Stay there. I'm coming right over."

When I drove into the driveway, she was standing in the front yard. It was a hot summer day. By then I was pretty steamed myself.

"Ok Julie, let's have this out right now. Did you or did you not tell me that if you couldn't sell you would just rent the house out? Yes or no?"

Silence. Head nod yes.

"And did you not tell me if the market changed you wouldn't drop your price? [Nod.] I told you I would not be calling you for a market update and not to blame me if you couldn't get that good price back again. Correct?" Another nod.

Silence. A final nod. I was on a tirade now.

"So now it looks like you have changed your mind. Now you want to sell, and you're mad at me for obeying your wishes. If you change your mind, you gotta tell me. I am not a mind reader, Julie. I only claimed to be an excellent realtor, not a mind reader! So don't be pissed off at me because I can't read your mind."

I was done.

"Yes Sharon, everything you said is right, and I'm sorry. I guess I'm just frustrated with everything. I am sorry. That wasn't fair."

"No, it sure wasn't. Now the question is, what are we going to do about the situation? Why don't we have a cup of tea and talk about it."

We went into the house together, and I told Julie to sit down and relax, and I would make the tea. We had a cookie too and decided to do whatever it would take to sell fast. They were completing on their new place soon, and time was flying by.

As I was leaving that day I said, "So Julie, are we ok?"

"Yes Sharon, we are. Thanks for coming over and not firing me." (Her exact words.)

In the end, we dropped their list price from $259,900 to $234,900 which was right in line with the new market value. They sold right away for $228,000. And guess what? The appliances were included this time with no argument! They had turned down $250,000. This was $22,000 less. Ouch!

Folks buying and selling real estate are often in a highly intense emotional state and require support to get through it. Pride, greed, love and fear are usually the main components of the stressful rollercoaster ride they may find themselves on. Sometimes I just listen, sometimes I give feedback and sometimes I have to match their intensity. But first I must manage myself and choose how to respond and not just react. Remember, we are the eye of the hurricane and the voice of understanding and reason, but first they have to calm down enough to hear and absorb reason.

This story was a perfect example of how a good person can "lose it." Prideful overconfidence, a dose of greed, and fear of being taken advantage of are all buttons being pushed, and suddenly a perfectly, lovely reasonable person can become an unreasonable, blaming, vindictive force of negative energy. I knew with Julie her behavior was her default way of showing up under stress. We all have one. She knew she had cost their family money because of her stubbornness and unreasonable attitude. In fact, she cost them $22,000. It was Julie's guilt. I assured her that she was still doing well on the deal considering what they had paid and how little they had invested in a little paint and some laminate flooring. They still made money on the house.

A little later that day of the encounter between Julie and me, an interesting thing happened. A long-time client of mine called me to make the following report:

(Ring…ring…)

"Hello, Sharon speaking."

"Hi Sharon, it's Marie."

"Hi Marie, how nice to hear from you."

"I just had a call from a friend, and I just had to call and tell you this story. My friend lives right next door to that listing of yours on Lilac Drive. She told me, 'Marie, you really should have heard this big argument next door. The house has been on the market for quite a while; your realtor Sharon Mason has it listed. Well she came over and tore a strip off my neighbour Julie. I had my windows open, and I really didn't mean to eavesdrop but I couldn't help it. They had this huge blow up and my neighbour ended up apologizing to Sharon. It was really something.'"

"Oh thanks Marie. I guess it's going to be a hot topic in the neighbourhood. It was pretty stressful, but we got it all ironed out and the house is going to sell now. Thanks for letting me know and please tell your friend that all is well."

At the end of the day, I did my job and got Julie and Ed's house sold. Julie was a bit of a real estate know-it-all, but I'm pretty sure that she learned her lesson. Julie's lesson: In a hot seller's market, take the money and run. It can all change in a heartbeat.

You might be wondering about dealing with a situation like that. At the time, it may seem that the likelihood of ever getting that property sold, and therefore the chance of getting paid, could be slim or none. Dealing with a client who does not respond reasonably to reason, and a mega stubborn one at that, might inspire thoughts of cancelling the listing and even choosing not to deal with the person at all. Here's another view of the situation: *my* view.

1. I have two clients here, not just Julie. There's Ed, who is reasonable. He's between a rock and a hard place. The mother of his children is having a meltdown, and he is walking a

fine line. I could not and would not abandon him. He wasn't saying much, wanting to keep some peace in the family.

2. I knew they had to sell. They had already bought. I also knew they were bluffing about renting the house out to tenants. Every time I have heard that during my career it has been a bluff. It's a go-to tactic when sellers are trying to get more for their property, and it's their right to get as much as the market will bear. Being a landlord can be a nightmare and an expensive one at that! There are tenants who don't pay the rent, or leave in the middle of the night and take your appliances with them or start a grow op….you never know unless you hire the right services. (Before you even think of being a landlord, or even if you are a landlord, you MUST talk to Jim and Anna Garnett at Canadian Tenant Inspection Services. [www.ctiservices.ca or 778-846-9125] You can thank me later.)

Anyway, back to Ed and Julie, I was patient with the process. I did what they wanted and let it play out. I knew that they would eventually have to sell. And I would be there to see it through with them no matter what came next. Julie would have to back down, and my job was to allow her to do that and make it ok that she messed up. I knew we would have to reduce the price. I wanted to keep the listing and, of course, get paid.

LIFE LESSON: Sensitivity, patience, taking the high road and knowing how to resolve a highly emotional conflict are people skills you need. Stand your ground as the adult you are. Tell the truth and make peace.

9

It's Complicated...Go Figure!

"I don't make things complicated.
That's the way they get all by themselves."
Mel Gibson

Someone recently asked me how a realtor distinguishes between a real client and a looky-loo. Let's define looky-loo. This particular species comes in many forms and can usually be found in their natural habitat: the open house.

Just for the record, there are four basic types of looky-loos: the sightseer, the dreamer, the nosy neighbour, and the wannabe.

1. The sightseer: One good example of the sightseers are the folks who don't have much to do on a Sunday afternoon, especially on a rainy day. I sometimes see sisters and female friends going to open houses together (and I always assume the guys are at home watching football). Also, there's always

123

the entertainment value of going to open houses. (A realtor can always tell if people are really investigating the market; they are sizing up what they could buy and also trying to get an idea of what they could sell for by comparing what they own with other properties for sale in the neighbourhood.) Really, it's probably just curiosity. These particular looky-loos will rarely engage with a realtor. They are normally in and out in a hurry, and they try not to even say hello and will avoid too much eye contact. The word I would apply to that species is "skittish." A realtor can spot them in a minute. It's like they feel guilty for being there under false pretences. They don't realize two things:

- As realtors, we don't mind. Just tell the truth.
- They are actually considering a move, otherwise they wouldn't be doing what they are doing. It may be a year or two away, but they are considering it somewhere in the back of their mind.

2. The dreamer: This is a delightful species of looky-loos who have "champagne taste and a beer budget" (like most of us). They love to come through the most expensive and brand-new homes and dream. I always hope they are working towards getting into the market or at least buying lottery tickets. The unfortunate thing here is that they are focusing on what they can't have. This can make it difficult for them to accept the reality of where they need to start out to gradually get that dream home or something like it. Also they love to look for decorating ideas in gorgeous homes, especially ones that are professionally staged. This dreamy tactic also works online. Many dreamers love to look at high-end homes online (especially if they have insomnia).

3. The nosy neighbour: This is one of my favourites. I am always charmed by the way they often tell me that they live

down the street and ask, "Is it ok if we take a look?" I love it when people just tell the truth. I get to find out about the neighbourhood, and I can also tell buyers that we have met a lot of the neighbours and what a pleasant group they are. (But only if it's true.)

4. The wannabe: These are often chatty, outgoing folks who are thinking of or wanting to be decorators, realtors, stagers or designers. They just love houses, furniture, drapes, blinds and garages, and would love to be more involved. They like to talk to realtors, to talk about houses, prices, the market or anything to do with real estate. Some are already involved as investors, designers, renovators and mortgage brokers. All are a welcome part of our world and community.

Psychologists suggest that everyone makes decisions every day as to whether they will keep doing what they are doing or make a change. Will I sell my house and buy another or quit my job and travel around the world with the money? Will I stay with my current spouse or significant other, or will I change my mind and run off with the circus or join a rock band? (I actually know people who have done similar things or have given them serious consideration.) These may just be fleeting thoughts, but they are pretty universal. So for the open house looky-loos, it may all still be subconscious, but it is bubbling below the surface. If you can engage them even a little, do it. You never know what you will find.

A lot of folks who come to open houses can and will become a source of business for realtors. Or at least they will want to have a realtor of their own if they don't already. So how do you separate the looky-loo from a possible client? The rubber meets the road the minute you introduce the 'm' word and start talking about money. In real estate it's all about the money and the math.

The most important thing I say to a new client, or even a past client, when we start to talk about moving is "Have you taken any steps to get prequalified?" What this means in plain English is "have you talked to a mortgage specialist about your financial situation and what you can afford and/or if you can afford the move you are thinking of making?" Until this step is complete, you cannot go forward at all.

Here's the rule of law when dealing with buyers: never, and I mean *never*, show property to buyers without a prequalification. That means the mortgage specialist has looked at their financial situation (income, debts, savings, credit rating…all documented of course) and told them what they can afford to buy. If they already own a property, that is also taken into consideration. The realtor has done a comparative market analysis (remember that?) to determine how much they will have flowing from the sale, and the mortgage specialist will work out how high they could go for their next purchase. Then, and only then, does the realtor know how to proceed or if to proceed.

For the first-time buyer, or the buyer who doesn`t have anything to sell, it is not clear what price range they can look at for their purchase. Without their being prequalified, I would have no idea what they could purchase and therefore no idea what properties I could show them that they could qualify to purchase. The major factor here is that the potential buyer needs a track record of having the income to qualify for a mortgage. They may not have a proper cash-down payment or may have such bad credit that they are too big a risk for a lender. (Just FYI, there are lenders out there who will lend to risky borrowers, but it is usually very costly with high interest rates and extra fees that can run into the thousands.)

That, boys and girls, is how we tell a looky-loo from a possible client: they are willing to get prequalified and talk money. Then, and only then, can we work with them. Makes sense, doesn't it?

LIFE LESSON: Everything is a process that has a correct way of approaching it. Do the steps in the right order, and do not make exceptions. That's always best for everyone; there are no short cuts to doing it right.

Here's a little more about open houses.

Meet Brent and Marilyn

A huge amount of my business over the decades has come from folks I met at open houses. A few years ago I had an exceptional house listed. Those dear clients Brent and Marilyn have both passed on now, but I will never forget the warm and history-filled property they let me help sell. They really needed to move to a one-level home. (No stairs for them please.) They loved their home intensely, and it was a hard, emotional time for them. The house was filled with a lifetime of memories, especially of their beloved golden cocker spaniel, Honey, who had just gone on to doggy heaven. They were referred to me by my mortgage broker, Sean.

Their love for their home and the sweet memories it contained made it very difficult for them to price it realistically in order to sell. Of course, they could not accept the true market value of the property, so it was a long, slow process of being on the market at a price that was too high and no offers coming in. They needed time for reality to set in and to lower the price to a realistic number. They were such wonderful people that I signed up for the long, emotional journey to get them moved. This meant at least one open house every weekend, maybe two.

The advantage of having an attractive feature-rich property like this one in a desirable location for an extended period of time is that one can meet a lot of prospective clients at the open houses. All kinds of looky-loos and non looky-loos flocked to see this wonderful house with its amazing garden, patio and entertainment areas. Not only that, Marilyn was an amazing homemaker, and every open house she would leave my husband and me a pot of delicious coffee and some homemade goodies to enjoy.

With Brent and Marilyn, even though I was always giving them not the best real estate news (like "no offers" and "the realtors say the price is too high"), their kindness never failed, and they always appreciated that I was just doing my job. They wanted to stay in denial as long as possible.

During the long listing period—almost five months—the contacts I made at open houses eventually turned into eleven sales, or eleven ends. (Remember ends? A listing sold or a purchase) Here's one example.

Meet Francis and Mike

At one of the open houses at Brent and Marilyn's, the doorbell rang and a very good-looking couple were standing there. They were obviously four or five months' pregnant.

"Can we look at the house?"

"Of course! Come right in! I'm Sharon and I'm the realtor. This is my hubby, Al. So go have a good look around, and then we can talk if you'd like."

They looked all around the house and came to talk. They were wondering what they could buy if they sold. Obviously they were having a baby, and they told us they had no yard where they were so were looking to move to a house. We gave them our brochure—"shameless self-promotion" as I confessed to them—and we said goodbye.

Several months later they called me.

(Ring…ring…)

"Hello, Sharon speaking."

"Hello Sharon. I don't know if you remember us. We came through your open house a few months ago. We were expecting our son at the time. He is about to arrive, and we are ready to think about moving. I'm Mike by the way."

"Oh, hello Mike. How nice to hear from you."

"So we've seen a house we want to buy, and we would like you to do the offer for us. Also, we're obviously needing to sell, and would you come and talk to us about that too?"

I did all of the above, and during the process they told me that they had been going around to open houses for a while looking for a realtor. They chose me. I was flattered beyond words. Those dear folks and their superior townhouse would end up accounting for four of those eleven ends.

THE LESSON: Treat everyone like gold. In the case of real estate, you never know why people are at an open house. Always assume they are looking for a realtor to work with.

One of the things I have loved in my real estate career are the challenges of finding ways to help my clients get what they want. It often requires very creative solutions. There are nuances and aspects to any transaction that can create opportunities for unusual and creative solutions to what appear to be obstacles.

Meet Brad and Charlotte

I had helped these very sharp and ambitious folks move in the past, so we had a strong relationship. Brad and Charlotte called me to talk about how they wanted to build their dream home. We decided the first step was to establish financing for this big project, find a nice big lot and buy it. Then we could start working on the plans and setting the wheels in motion to find a good builder and get the ball rolling on all the red tape to obtain a building permit. (It's a project!) Their plan was to sell their current home and rent until the new home was ready for occupancy.

Once all that was under way, we got their current property on the market as they would need the cash out of their present home to put towards the new one. We went on the market for $469,000. It was a lovely three-bedroom house that looked like a show home (what we realtors in those days called "a peach"). Towards the end of the second open house, a super nice Chinese realtor came in with his buyer in tow. The buyer was a highly unusual person who truly wore his heart and his thoughts on his sleeve. He loved the property and wanted to buy it.

He spoke directly to me, "I want to buy this house, and I'm not leaving until I do."

Hmmm, never had anyone say that before. My delightful realtor colleague smiled and winked at me as if to say "Go for it."

"Oh, I see. Well my clients should be home soon. Why don't you sit down at the dining room table and write up an offer."

They did. In those days, an offer was one page, written or printed by hand. Six copies with carbon paper. If you've never heard of carbon paper, ask someone in an older generation. Today, in 2022, if I write an offer for a buyer, it can be up to seven or eight pages with up to another seven pages of government red tape. Thankfully it is all done online now, and carbon paper is just a distant memory!

When my sellers came home, I set up for the negotiation by having the potential buyer and his realtor in the living room and my sellers in the kitchen with me. We were expecting to sell the home in the $450,000 to $460,000 range. The offer was $430,000. Not enough. My sellers' position on that price was an absolutely no.

I took the buyer's agent aside.

"This offer is pretty low."

"Yes, I know, but he won't go higher."

"So what are his plans? Is he going to live in the house or what?"

"No, he's going back to China and would maybe rent it out or leave it empty." A person could do that in those days. Not so much now. New rules, new taxes.

"Oh I see…" Then was one of those moments when a light bulb goes on over your head: an idea!

"Yeah, I think he doesn't really care about the money, and maybe tenants could be a problem…you know, him being so far away and everything."

"Yes, I understand. Let me see what I can do."

I went back to my sellers armed with my new idea (maybe it was even a flash of brilliance; time would tell). I suggested to my sellers that we might make a deal where the buyer would close the transaction (in plain English: pay for the house) and let them stay in the house rent free for a year. That way they would not be out of pocket for a year of rent, and they would have their cash on hand to start construction. They would also be able to avoid moving twice, avoid property taxes or insurance on the house for a year and avoid fees for hooking up heat, electricity, cable and other details at the rental house. AND the kids could stay in their current school for another year.

It was all about the math.

I showed them how the value of an offer is not always confined to the price. There are other factors that can have a bigger value to a seller than just money. In this case the big attraction was not having to endure the distraction of finding a rental, moving twice and uprooting everything and gaining the beauty of living rent free for a year with no pressure to get the new house finished and get moved. And no more showing their current home and hoping for an offer. It was a sweet deal for them in so many ways.

The buyer agreed to everything, and everyone was happy. In fact, my seller was amazed that they ended up with a much happier transaction than they could have imagined.

THE LESSON: As a realtor we deal with property, bricks and mortar and buildings and land, but the real thing we are dealing with are *people's circumstances*.

I learned this from my dad many years before I ever thought of being a realtor. He used to talk to me about his work as a realtor, and so much of what he said stuck with me. In this case, it was a matter of matching up two sets of circumstances so that it worked. Think of a jigsaw puzzle and imagine the circumstances as pieces that can fit perfectly together. It was extremely satisfying to put that transaction together for my clients. Always remember, if you can satisfy their circumstances, you are well on your way to having happy clients. And that, of course, is the only time we get paid.

Meet George and Hazel

This kind and gentle couple were referred to me by a precious friend and colleague; the late, legendary realtor Johnny Armeneau.

George and Hazel had an exceptional little house located in a private cul-de-sac. It was one of those high-rated, energy-efficient houses, so was very well built and well insulated. A solid home.

They were in their late sixties and retired at the time. George had to go to a hospital every day for dialysis due to kidney disease, and Hazel was in the early stages of Alzheimer's. And George wasn't going to be able to drive much longer.

George and Hazel had been working with Johnny, and he had located the one and only condo that could fulfill their very specific needs. It was a bright and pleasant corner condo that was an easy walk to a hospital with a dialysis unit and across the street from an adult daycare where he could safely leave Hazel while he was having his daily treatment. It was ideal and like finding a needle in a haystack. To locate a property in the right price range that could satisfy such specific needs is what I call a real estate miracle.

They had an offer in place on this condo. It was "subject to the sale" of their house. This was a case where they couldn't sell before they found just the right place to fit with their circumstances. They needed to know for sure that they were going to a place where they could live out their days.

Ah yes, always dealing with people's circumstances. And these circumstances were not negotiable.

So here's the problem we were facing. In the case of a subject-to-sale offer there is always something called a "time clause." A time clause says that if the seller receives another offer, it doesn't have to be for more money, they are free to sell to that party. BUT they first must give the current purchaser a chance to step up and make a commitment to buying the property. Hence the time clause allows the current buyer to have a day or so to remove that subject-to-sale clause, or they have to step aside and let the new buyer have the property. That meant that when I listed George and Hazel's place, we needed to get it sold before someone else made an offer on the only place available that totally worked for them. And you know what that meant: pricing it right.

We met and I told them that I would do everything in my power to get them that condo. I also told them that there is a price to make any property sell in a day. I also said, "We're not going there yet, but we can if we have to."

This was a case where money was not the number one consideration. What they needed in order to deal with their health concerns was far more important than money. Once they sold, they could easily live on their pensions, and anything from the house would be gravy. (But never mind, I was going to get them every penny I could.)

We went on the market at $239,900. I expected them to sell close to that. I had the realtor tour through, and realtors from all the companies in their area had a chance to see the house on the Wednesday after we went on the market. Three days later, the axe fell. Johnny let me know that the seller of that one-and-only perfect condo had received another offer, and they had just invoked the dreaded time clause. Fortunately we had forty-eight hours to get George and Hazel's place sold before they would lose the condo. I rushed to their house and gave them the scary news.

"So, Sharon, what about that price you said where we could sell in a day?" George had been listening.

"That would be $199,000. And people would come with lower offers. They would see it's a fire sale."

"Ok, let's do it."

"George, I have another idea." It was ten in the morning on day one, and we had a bit of time on our side. "Let's see if we can motivate the realtors to bring us a good offer. Let's drop the price and offer the realtor who sells the house a $5,000 bonus. And let's say they have 'til 5 p.m. today." I knew that was our best shot. We didn't have enough time to publish a new lower price on the multiple listing service and get an offer that way.

"Ok Sharon, what should we drop the price to?"

"$219,900."

"Ok, where do we sign?"

I had a price reduction form with me, and I added in the comments that there was a $5,000 bonus to the buyer's agent. Then I quickly printed up a flyer announcing the new price and the bonus and had it circulated to all the real estate offices in the area. I made it clear that we needed it sold immediately and that the offer could have no "subject to" clause on it at all. Then I did the most important thing of all: I personally called all the realtors who came through on the realtors' tour and filled them in on the situation. And I did something else that is always a great strategy in a pinch: I called the agents in the area who were the busiest (selling the most homes). They could easily have buyers looking for a nice two-bedroom rancher for sale at a great price.

In today's digital world, we realtors would also be using an app called Touchbase. In a situation like George and Hazel's, we can send a message to the many with the touch of a button. New technology is allowing us to serve our clients more effectively than ever.

Sure enough, around 4 p.m. that day my phone rang, and a realtor had an offer. We sold that sweet property for $218,000. My clients were thrilled and relieved. In this case, it was all about the circumstances, and it was all about a creative solution. This was actually a real estate emergency. It's the only real estate emergency I have ever been involved in, and I hope it's the last.

THE LESSON: Always prepare yourself and your client for the worst-case scenario. Bring your expertise and great strategies. It's called "whatever it takes!"

LIFE LESSON: There's always a way. And there's always a lesson.

In this case, knowing ahead of time that we could sell in a day if we had to made all the difference. For the folks who wrote the second offer on the condo, the worst-case scenario for them would be that they could not get the condo because the folks with the first offer in place might remove their subject-to-sale clause. And in this case George and Hazel did. Often those first people to place the offer can't remove the clause.

One the realtors I had talked to called me to see if we had sold George and Hazel's house. When I filled him in on the story, his comment was "Well Sharon, you pulled a rabbit out of a hat on that one." I guess I pretty much did!

A few words about Johnny Armeneau: In my real estate board, the greatest honour for any realtor is to receive the John Armeneau Award, which recognizes the outstanding contribution of a realtor to the industry and to our immediate real estate community. Whenever my phone would ring around 10 p.m., it was usually Johnny giving me a referral. It always went like this:

(Ring…ring…)

"Hello. Sharon speaking."

"Hello beautiful child of the universe."

"Hello John. Lovely to hear from you. You still working?"

"Yup."

"Me too. What can I do for you?"

Then he would give me the details of the clients we were teaming up to help. (And that's how I met George and Hazel.) Johnny left us much too soon, and I miss him every day.

MORE LESSONS: Always be professional and treat each person

in your path with kindness and respect and in a spirit of service. Relationships are everything, with your clients, your colleagues and members of the public.

Before we leave this chapter, let's spend a little more time on the topic of whether to sell first or buy first. We just saw an example of that in the case of George and Hazel. They were people who had to know for sure what they are moving to, but in most cases it's not a must-know situation. The major concern in this area is that when people decide it's time to make a move, many are afraid that they won't be able to find what they want. They have no vision of what is in store. It feels like jumping out of a plane with no parachute.

I explain it to my clients like this: imagine you are a trapeze artist. You have firm grasp on your current trapeze grip bar. Of course, you feel like you cannot let go until you can at least see the one from the other side coming towards you. The client has to have an idea that there will be something to grab onto once they let go.

My job as their realtor is to educate them about what their choices will be in dealing with this issue. The most common factor is that they need the money from the sale of their current home (commonly called "the proceeds of the sale") in order to pay for their new home. It's all about the math, and this is the reality of the situation.

Let's say it's a client who must buy first; they simply cannot and will not live with the uncertainty factor. It's just too stressful and too terrifying. They must understand some things about that choice. So they see the "perfect property." Great. They now have two choices.

The first choice is to put in an offer on the "perfect property" with a subject-to-sale clause. Their only hope of getting this offer accepted is if they are already listed for sale at an attractive price. We already know too well the possible pitfalls of doing that from the case of George and Hazel, including being faced with that pesky time clause. You know that another offer could show up and dash your hopes and dreams if you haven't sold yet. Also, since you want to get that "perfect property," you are now more motivated to sell quickly, so you may have to reduce your asking price to get more activity, and you may be tempted to sell for less than you could have. In a case like that, the client is motivated by FOMO: fear of missing out. This can be just as stressful as selling first.

If that scenario is not attractive to the client, the other alternative is bridge financing. Let's say, for example, the client hasn't sold yet and finds a perfect property. They can go ahead and purchase it before they have sold if a lender will finance it. Let's say the lender is a bank. So they speak to their friendly banker to see if they can borrow the entire amount on the home they wish to purchase. Their current home is still on the market, not sold and with no certainty of if or when it will. So far it looks saleable; the price is good, realtors are bringing people through and they have a mortgage on that house as well. The idea is that once the current home sells, the new home would be paid for with the proceeds of that sale. BUT what if the home never sells? What if the market changes or interest rates go up all of a sudden? What if someone lost their job? Those clients could end up with two houses and two mortgages. It can be difficult to qualify for two mortgages at the same time depending on the size of the mortgages and the value of the properties involved.

This process of buying first can be a minefield, however it depends on many factors and may make good sense at time. The trick is knowing when it makes sense and when the risk factors are possibly too high.

One situation where buying first makes sense is in buying a "presale." A presale is where the house, condo or townhouse is under construction or maybe not even started yet (often just a big hole in the ground). There are risks here (like everything in life), and there are never any guarantees, so due diligence is always required. However, folks can often buy a presale at a good price. The property may not be completed for months or even years. It requires a deposit, usually a series of deposits, and the completion date will be determined closer to the completion of the project. Going forward, the client has lots of time to sell and make any arrangements needed to accommodate an uncertain move-in date for their new home. The main thing for a realtor to remember is to always disclose all the possible things that can go wrong along with all the potential benefits of any of the decisions to be made.

How I like to deal with the sell-first-or-buy-first dilemma is to go over the alternatives and explain the choices available if one buys first. They need to understand fully about "subject to sale" and "bridge financing." And then I make this suggestion: "In the meantime, why don't I get the ball rolling to list your property? We have some staging to do, and we have lots of paperwork, measuring and so on. Why don't I set up a search of listings and send you any properties that may be a good fit for you. You can drive by, look at all the photos, and read all about them. We can pick out some for us to see together in person. I need to get a good idea of what you are dreaming of so that I know what we're looking for. But you have to promise me one thing. It's a rule of mine: no falling in love with a home until the day you move in. Because here's the problem, you may likely find the perfect home too soon...before you have sold. Always remember that there is always another home, and it's usually even better than the one you didn't get. You really need to see what's out there. After we have done all this, if you aren't comfortable, we can take your home off the market. No problem."

Once we have gone through the reality check on buying first and started the looking process, I have rarely seen the issue continue. And I always tell my clients that if push comes to shove, we will sell their property with a new twist: subject to them buying. I have had buyers of my listings and their realtors agree to this strategy which was totally in favour of my sellers who needed a couple of weeks to solidify the purchase of a new home.

It is almost always better to sell first and, once the sale is guaranteed in writing, to go out and buy from a position of strength. I tell them that once we know their home is sold and completing on a certain date in the future, all I do twenty-four hours a day is finding them that ideal home.

THE LESSON: Helping our clients get there takes patience, understanding and the ability to educate them to the realities. Take them by the hand and empower them with understanding and knowledge. That is how we become their realtor for life.

10

The Love and the Lessons...
Claiming Your Space

"Good judgement comes from experience, and a lot of that comes from bad judgement."
Will Rogers

Success, each person has their own personal definition of the word. For me, after a journey of decades, I have a perspective that includes many moving parts.

Trial and error is clearly the most common learning model, but if you can learn from other people's experiences you are ahead of the game.

My best advice is basic. Figure out what you believe in. What are your principles? What do you stand for? What is your philosophy that gets you through the hard times and keeps you going? What creates the resilience in you that will carry you to your personal definition of success?

As you go forward in real estate or anything in life—in business, in families, in sports or any aspect of life—these questions remain the same. They are big questions that are key to the character of a human being, which is the key to the experience we create for ourselves here on Earth.

I have found many authors and thought leaders who have helped me find my way to a path that has given me great success, both personally and financially. One of my favourites is the late Steven Covey. You can never go wrong following his principles. I'm offering my three favourites here and taking some poetic licence of my own. One of his best-selling books *The Seven Habits of Highly Successful People* is a must-read, followed by his sequel *The Eighth Habit*.

1. "Always begin with the end in mind." What do I want this relationship to look like five years and ten years from now? As a realtor, when I meet with a new client, I am always conscious of that principle. My "end" is never to "get a paycheque." My "end in mind" is to establish a relationship that lasts until one of us dies. My end is to earn their trust and to be there if they need to sell, buy or just ask a question such as "What did the house next door to me sell for?" or "Can you tell me what they are asking for the house down the street?" or "What are two-bedroom condos selling for [in a certain area]?" My intention is to earn the right to ask for referrals when they have someone near to them who needs to talk to a realtor. The end I have in mind is one that offers multiple opportunities to be of service for the long term. I'm here for the duration and at your service.

2. "Win-win or no deal." Always do the right thing. I believe that fairness to everyone is the only way to go, in life and in business. I believe that everyone should get paid

142

for their work. And I know that what goes around comes around.

Before we get to the third of my favourite principles, here's a real-life example of always seeking win-win deals and doing the right thing.

Meet Roger and Serena

I met Roger at an open house I did for Frances and Mike. (Remember them from Chapter 9? They were expecting their son.) Roger really loved the townhouse and would have loved to make an offer, but the problem was it was age restricted, and that wouldn't do for their family. Roger was from Taiwan, and I have to confess that my Mandarin is non-existent (as all my Asian clients know). He was apologizing for his English, which was hugely superior to my Mandarin. We managed to communicate with lots of smiling and gestures, and we even exchanged phone numbers and decided to connect to see if I could help him and his family find a home to purchase.

As I got to know Roger, I saw what a sweet, kind and smart fellow he was and is. His wife Serena, a sharp cookie if I ever saw one, knew exactly what she was looking for. There was a townhouse complex that had one-level homes, very attractive for them, and no age restrictions. Also a major feature for them: a gated community. I went and looked it up right away to see if there was anything for sale. No such luck. I checked on expired and cancelled listings in case someone had wanted to sell and didn't. There was just one. It checked all the boxes. It had not expired; they had cancelled it. That usually means that either they had a change of plans, or they just got tired of being on the market and gave up trying to sell.

The point I'm making here is that, at this point, I could have called the owner myself and asked if they still wanted to sell. Then I could have listed that property and had Roger and Serena buy it. I could have...but I didn't. Here's what I decided was the right thing to do. I called the realtor who had it listed when it was cancelled. I wanted to give him a chance to get paid for his work. It can be a lot of effort and time to get a property on the market (expense, research, paperwork and more). Here's what happened.

(Ring…ring…)

"Hello?"

"Hello, is that Bill?"

"Yes this is Bill speaking."

"Hi Bill. This is Sharon Mason from HomeLife Benchmark Titus Realty. I have some clients interested in Sunnydale Gardens. You had a listing there a few months ago, and I'm wondering if your clients would still be interested in selling. I think it might be a good fit."

"Who are you again?"

I repeated myself.

"And you're calling *me*?" ("Me" as in "not them.")

"Yes, I don't want to be calling your clients. You've put in a lot of effort, and I believe that we should all get paid for our hard work. If the place is clean and shows well, I think my buyers would go for it."

"Well, I've never had a call like this before. Thanks for calling me. I'll talk to them and get back to you."

I think he was in shock. As a rule, realtors go after expired and cancelled listings and try to get the listing (get the seller back on the market under their banner). The implication is that the original listing agent was somehow delinquent in their duties to the seller in giving the wrong advice or not taking enough photos or some other shortcoming. Sometimes the seller just simply has a change of heart. They may have had offers that didn't fly for various reasons: a buyer couldn't get a mortgage or a buyer lost their job all of a sudden. Lots of things can happen.

Calling Bill, for me, was playing win-win. The Golden Rule. I would love to get a call like mine in a parallel situation. Let's help everyone get paid for their hard work. Let's take a moment here to talk about the important issue of something called "agency."

That particular situation with Bill happened a few years ago when, in my marketplace, it was permitted for a realtor to have a listing and sell it to their own buyer. The realtor was, in fact, representing both the seller and the buyer at the same time. That is called "double-ending" a listing. If you stop to think about it, there is a big conflict of interest inherent in that practice. The most common situation for selling a property is when there are two realtors and their two real estate brokerages involved: one represents the interests of the seller, and one represents the interests of the buyer. The real estate fee is then split between the two companies and the two real estate agents. Not so if there is only one realtor representing both parties. And here's where the conflict arises. That double-ending realtor gets to keep the *entire real estate fee* for him or herself.

My view of double-ending is that you cannot truly serve two masters. Here's the question that must be asked: Who is that realtor really working for? Maybe the answer is that he or she is working for him or herself. Yes, the realtor in question is doing the work of two realtors and keeping twice the money, but do the two clients—the seller and the buyer—really have undivided loyalty from that one agent? Do they really understand what they agreed to in having one realtor working for both parties? And what is the underlying motivation of that realtor? It's a question of ethics, and that is why the practice of double-ending has undergone changes in many jurisdictions.

These days, in my marketplace, the rules have changed. If we decide to represent a buyer for our own listing, the buyer must sign documents agreeing to and acknowledging the fact that the listing realtor is working for the seller only, as the seller's agent, and the buyer has to acknowledge that they do not have their own realtor to advise and protect them and keep their secrets. They are totally on their own, and they are called an "unrepresented party." This is a good thing that buyers are now properly protected as real estate consumers. They are strongly warned and advised to choose to be represented by a licensed professional real estate agent. (Imagine a lawyer trying to represent both sides in a lawsuit!)

Respecting "agency" can be a slippery slope. My brokerage does not allow us to work with unrepresented parties, and I would never attempt it anyway. Too many things can go wrong, and I don't agree with the concept of double-ending in principle. Each party deserves, and very much needs, independent representation not tainted by anyone's self-interest. It's about something called "pure intention" which says "I am here to serve the best interests of others." It's a tall order for some folks to set aside their own financial and ego needs, but obeying the true meaning of agency requires this commitment.

A lot of realtors would have tried to get Bill's old listing and double-end it to Roger and Serena. As you know, in the case of a realtor double-ending a listing, the realtor would not have to share the real estate fee with a second agent. That agent would earn almost twice as much on that one transaction. That's why Bill was so surprised by my call. It was not my agenda to cut him out of the deal. It turned out his former seller didn't want to sell after all, however I had the opportunity to "do the right thing" according to my philosophy, in line with the Golden Rule and in line with my principles and values. When you know what those are, decisions become easy.

About two weeks later, the perfect place in that complex came on the market and we pounced immediately. Roger and Serena have owned happily there for eight years.

Back to my list of three favourite principles.

3. "Sharpen the axe." This principle is all about balance and self-care. Here's a tale that illustrates this important point.

   There were two big, rough-and-tough lumberjacks Jack and Mack who were always competing with each other to see who was the toughest, the strongest. They decided to finally settle their rivalry by having a contest to see which one could chop down the most trees in four hours. There were judges and spectators present, and when the starter blew his whistle, they both went at it with a fury. After the first forty-five minutes, Jack disappeared from the scene for about ten minutes. Then he reappeared and kept chopping. After an hour he did it again; gone for about ten minutes. He repeated this pattern regularly for the four hours. Meanwhile, Mack was continuously hacking and hewing. At the end of the four hours—you guessed it—Jack had chopped down considerably more trees than Mack. Mack was totally flummoxed.

"How on earth did you do that Jack? I don't get it. You kept leaving, and I worked the whole time. Where'd you go? What were you doing?"

Of course you know his answer. "I was sharpening my axe."

The point here is the importance of taking care of yourself. You see, I once was that ambitious, hard-working, driven person with big dreams. Be careful what you wish for. I, in fact, got what I wished for—a huge real estate practice. The phone was ringing for me constantly, and I had huge responsibilities and often over a hundred items a day to deal with. I had created a monster. And here's the kicker: that monster needed to be fed, and I was the food.

Ultimately, we got smarter. In the early days, my dear husband Al and I would go away for two weeks, and I would spend the first three days sleeping. (That was a sign.) Eventually we learned that you start your year by planning your holidays. Gurus will tell you all kinds of time-off plans, like two or three two-week holidays and four long weekends a year. That would be a plan for a very busy realtor who could then afford to pay for all that.

Find what works for you. Sometimes a week at a silent retreat is more than you need, and three weeks at a resort isn't enough. Discover what sharpens your axe—a spa day, meditation, a weekly massage, running, hiking or playing with the kids—and then do it. Be committed and make it, and you, a priority. (I've had burn out twice, and I don't recommend it.)

We all have energy reserves within us. It's hardwired into our nervous system. It's there for emergencies such as surviving a war, a siege or an ice age (as our Cro-Magnon ancestors did). It's there for those hard experiences life can throw at us. (I often think it's for parents and especially mothers who go without sleep for months, and even years, when the kids are babies.) Here's the thing: if you dip too deeply into your reserves, too often it can be almost impossible to restore them.

As a colleague of mine reported, "I lost my health to gain my fortune, and it cost me my fortune to regain my health."

Create your definition of success with *balance* as a major component. That must never be negotiable.

Let's talk about ceilings (and not just the glass ones), and how, as we have seen, people tend to have a comfort zone that can be hard to break through.

Once I figured some stuff out and learned how to be realtor, and once I realized I was pretty good at it, I started to dream bigger. I was not prepared to settle for an average income in a profession that offered so much more. I was in a company that recognized not only production, such as how many sales or dollar earnings in a year, but also personal growth, balance and contribution. They called it, and rightfully so, the Master Associate Program.

This program was based on consistent production and contribution to both the real estate community and the community at large. I liked that idea. It acknowledged the flow of giving and receiving. Life is nothing without that. My company Realty World had that unusual awareness of the personal and spiritual aspects of what real success means. This program recognized those of us who saw success as more than money. I can attest to the fact that the more I contributed to my industry and my greater community, the more financial success I enjoyed. (Funny how that works! The law of attraction: make friends with this law ASAP!)

For many consecutive years, I fulfilled all of the requirements for the Master Associate Designation: consistent high production as a realtor, volunteer work, training courses, participation in local events, and attending conventions and sales meetings. All of these had to be documented and authorized and sent to head office on a deadline. It kept me on my toes. It was an all-around good citizenship program; our democracy can always use more of that. (No kidding.)

Realty World Canada sent me on a tour of Western Canada to speak to Realty World offices. It was really fun. I travelled with a group of Realty World executives. We went to Winnipeg, Saskatoon, Edmonton, Calgary and, of course, ended up speaking in Vancouver to the BC realtors and brokers. I loved it.

Eventually I was notified that I had earned the Life Master Associate Designation, and I was invited to the Realty World International Convention in Las Vegas to receive my award. (I had attended it before, and it was big!) It turned out my dad could be with us on that trip, and we had a blast. (It was about a month before he died.) At that particular convention, for the first night they put on a "fun night." People had to go as their favourite celebrity. We were so busy with business before we left that I had no costume, and neither did Al. Dad, on the other hand, was all prepared to go as his all-time favourite Charlie Chaplin. That night, Al and I used what we had on hand and fit into the spirit of the party full of phony celebrities; I went as an autograph hound, and Al took his amazing camera and went as a paparazzi!

While we had a ball playing our parts with the "celebrities," Dad was busy being the silent movie legend: the signature walk-waddle exactly as Charlie did, the antics with his cane, his giant white handkerchief the size of a flag jammed in to his breast pocket which he took out with a flourish to dust off a perfectly clean chair by beating it to death before sitting down in his own dusty "tramp" costume. He had everyone in stitches as he "did" Charlie all evening! When it came time to give the prize for the best celebrity look alike, the whole room was chanting, "Char-lie! Char-lie! Char-Lie!" And, of course, he won! What a great memory we made. The next year Al and I went back for the next convention. When we approached the registration table we were immediately recognized, but not for ourselves. Everyone at the table wanted to know "Where's Charlie?" We had to tell them he was gone. It hurt. Sigh…

At one of our conventions, our little thirty-five-person office in Richmond, BC, Canada, received the top office award for North America. Our production volume even had to be reduced to US dollars, which is often the go-to currency worldwide. (And the Realty World home base was in the USA.) Our Realty World franchise office beat out American offices that had double and triple the number of agents. We became Realty World Rock Stars, and it felt like winning the Super Bowl or, in Canada, the Stanley Cup.

On another Realty World Las Vegas trip, I found myself invited to a special cocktail party to acknowledge a special achievement. I had been in the top one hundred agents in a company of 19,000 realtors for a decade. Oh my! My little dreams of an extra $20,000 a year seemed so touching and distant. It was the accumulation of all my hard work and personal development, all the late nights, all the miles I had put on my car, all the clients I had served, all the problems I had solved and all the uncomfortable risks I had endured. (I thought back to Mary Elias and my first little farm.) There I was attending an Inner Circle Reception with all the Super Stars, and I guess I was one of them!

I met all the company brass, and they were warm and wonderful. I was extremely humbled and grateful beyond words, grateful to my husband Al, my loyal clients and my company and colleagues who became family in so many ways. Then there was Harold Waddell, the owner of Realty World Canada and a crony of my dad from back in the day when they were in their prime as movers and shakers of the real estate scene in BC and in Canada.

What a journey it has been!

I had done the work, taken the risks, expanded my comfort zone, learned so many lessons and exceeded my wildest expectations. I had not only grown personally but also grown up and matured in ways I never could have as a "civilian"—my term for anyone who has never been in the real estate "trenches." I indeed made a life and a living serving my clients, my community, and my family.

For the Love of Real Estate

It is my hope that my stories and experiences
will inspire and support you along your own
real estate journey whether as a realtor or a confident,
informed buyer or seller of real estate.
Sharon

About the Author

Sharon Mason was born an entrepreneur. She grew up watching her dad go from rags to riches as a realtor, broker and land developer and, by osmosis, absorbed many lessons and attitudes that, years later, supported her many successes. In her younger years she became an honour student, a graduate of the University of Victoria and a member of the Royal Winnipeg Ballet, performing for Her Majesty Queen Elizabeth and the late Prince Phillip. Later, she took on the roles of teacher, wife, mother, homemaker, marathon runner, counsellor and now a published author. All this diverse experience helped pave the way for what was to come.

Sharon became a realtor in 1984 thinking that an extra $20,000 a year would make a huge difference to her family. Little did she know that embracing a journey of hard work, perseverance and personal growth would make her a superstar and a better person. Sharon quickly became a member of the Greater Vancouver Real Estate Board's prestigious Medallion Club and received Realty World's top designations—"Star Salesmaster" and "Master Associate." In fact, she maintained her spot in the top 100 agents among 18,000 Realty World realtors in North America for a decade. Many people speak of her as a real estate legend. Sharon reports that her long-time friend and colleague, Eric Wolf, told her one Monday morning, "Sharon—you're a real estate weapon!" This after, as a new realtor, she had posted five new sales on the office blackboard over a two-day weekend. Weapon indeed! As Sharon's practice grew, the new and repeat business and referrals came pouring in. The goal of $20,000 per year became a reality very quickly and far exceeded that amount. "I never dreamed I would be able to help so many people and make such a difference AND change our finances so much!"

These days Sharon loves to help her clients experience a level of care and service second to none and says that her goal is to make each transaction a "work of art" and as low stress as possible for buyers and sellers. She is proud to be a mentor to new realtors and works with her daughter, Justine Priestley, and her husband of forty-five years, Al Mason, their administrator who is humorously known far and wide as their "chauffeur." Sharon is delighted to share her insights, experiences and wisdom along with her sense of humour and story-telling genius in this long-awaited volume. She says, "It's part of my legacy, and I am grateful beyond words to share what I can with my readers, my community and my family, especially my children, Jason Priestley and Justine Priestley, and beloved grandchildren, Ava and Dashiell Priestley."

Sharon lives in Cloverdale, British Columbia, with her husband, Al Mason.

sharonmasonrealestate@gmail.com

www.SharonMasonRealEstate.com

The Author's Inspiration

After much consideration, I decided to dedicate this book to my father, the late Lorrace Eric Kirk, aka "Lorrie." He led the way as the first entrepreneur in the Kirk family and was a big inspiration into who I am today as a real estate agent and as a person of integrity and ethics. Dad was born in 1922 and right from the start he brought his unusual light into the world. He was a born entertainer and somehow his mother Trudie Kirk (nee Killips), my beloved late grandmother, saw his inborn talent. By the age of five he was a miniature song and dance "man" in vaudeville, performing regularly at the Pantages Theatre in Edmonton, his birthplace as well as mine. I have been told that he even opened for Charlie Chaplin back in the day.

As a young nineteen-year-old dad with a new baby—me—he took up his post in the Royal Canadian Navy learning to be a radio and radar specialist in order to help defend us all during World War II. Dad was doing "the Murmansk Run" in a convoy that sailed from Halifax, Nova Scotia, to Murmansk, Russia, carrying vital cargo for the war effort. In honouring him, and all those who have sacrificed everything, I always vote and proudly wear my poppy every November. Those of us whose lives have been touched by a world war have already passed on or soon will be, so I encourage the younger generations to study the past so that the human race does not have to repeat it quite so often.

When the war was over, Dad came home to Edmonton, and my parents happily moved us to Victoria, BC. I was two years old, and I remember it clearly. Throughout my early childhood, Dad always had his own business. He first fixed radios—a trade he learned while in the Navy. (Very old-school skills nowadays for sure.) Next Dad started a delivery service which he called, "The Coast Messenger." He bought a truck and started doing pick-ups and deliveries—a 1940s version of FedEx. In the late 40s, Dad, by some magical destiny, came across the opportunity to become a real estate agent. I recall that he bought a real estate licence for $2.50 or some insane-sounding amount! I think all you needed was a pulse and $2.50! He had both. Today it takes a lot more than that!

Being a smart guy with his eye on changing his family's story—breaking the mould, if you will—Dad got himself into a position of influence. The long and the short of it was that he ended up owning his first real estate company called "Northwestern Securities" on the corner of Yates and Broad streets in Victoria in the 1950s with his friend and partner, J. Donald Smith. Don was an influencer as a cabinet minister in the B.C. Social Credit government of W.A.C. "Wacky" Bennett, and between the two of them, they were instrumental in the birth of the Real Estate Act.

Dad could see what a great and important service properly licensed realtors could provide to the public. He also saw that the current unregulated situation was unacceptable in terms of ethical issues and protection of the public. Indeed, whenever large sums of money are on the menu, the absolute worst can be brought out in some folks. Real estate is one of those areas where temptation is around every corner, and Dad's idea was to raise being a realtor to a "profession." He and his partner Don went a long way to making it so. They a saw an opportunity to pave the way by "cleaning up" the unregulated world of selling and buying property. What a great legacy!

Dad was the president of the Greater Victoria Real Estate Board for many years, and he served in the Canadian Real Estate Association as well. He was involved in bringing the Multiple Listing Service to us and eventually opened the first real estate office in a shopping mall in Canada: Kirk's Mayfair Realty in the Mayfair Shopping Centre in Victoria. He became a land developer and, at the same time, became a member of the first graduating class from UBC as a Fellow of the Real Estate Institute, the coveted FRI designation. He became real estate royalty.

For a man who married my mother at age nineteen with $5 in his pocket, Dad came a long way. He wasn't home a lot, but he never missed any of my ballet recitals, Christmas concerts, plays or festival performances. He was my fan. His full story has never been told, but from what I know of it, it's what I like to call "the Canadian dream." It`s the same as "the American dream" but in Canadian dollars.

Dad had a bunch of high school buddies who had something like a pact. They had all grown up during the Great Depression of the 1930s. They had witnessed and experienced terrible poverty and decided they were going to do whatever it took to be financially successful, and they all were. Two of Dad`s famous school chums from Victoria High School in Edmonton were the wonderful actor Leslie Neilson (who made me laugh so hard it hurt) and the director Arthur Hiller who directed "Love Story" (which made me cry) as well as many other films and TV shows. You can still see his credits on reruns of shows like "Alfred Hitchcock Presents."

In Dad`s pursuit of success and significance, he discovered the renowned motivational speaker Earl Nightingale. Earl`s inspiring message is still available and is still as relevant today as it was then. Dad would talk to me about what he was learning that would ultimately change his life and destiny and, thankfully, mine.

"We become what we think about most often."

That is the basic message and the legacy of Earl Nightingale. That is what he was teaching my dad—and, by osmosis, me—way back when. Just goes to show us that there is nothing new under the sun. I still have the old 78 RPM plastic record of Earl`s message that Dad used to listen to over and over on the record player, now called a turntable. It`s the power of positive thinking. The message is always the same. Thoughts are things.

Today they call it "self-talk."

Dad was not a person without problems, challenges and even

personal demons, but I knew he always did his best. His motives were coming from the right place, and his contribution was enormous. Only as an older adult do I catch a glimpse of who he was and what his journey means.

Dad lived with Al and me for a month shortly before his passing at age seventy-one. Way too soon. I was blessed to have resolved the areas of conflict or discomfort in our relationship, which certainly had its stormy chapters in the past. No family seems to escape some kind of drama, and mine was no different.

Thanks Dad. You gave me great gifts. I would give anything for one more hour with you.

Sharon's father in his Canadian Navy uniform—1943